Paperbacks USA & UK Vol 2

BRITISH GANGSTER & EXPLOITATION PAPERBACKS OF THE POSTWAR YEARS

by Maurice Flanagan

ZEON BOOKS

1997

ISBN 1-874113-08-4

Cover by Perl from the Grant Hughes Paperback "Dangerous Dames"

ISBN 1-874113-08-4 British Gangster & Exploitation Paperbacks of the Postwar Years first published in 1997 by Zeon Books, an associate company of Zardoz Books, 20 Whitecroft, Dilton Marsh, Westbury, England, BA13 4DJ.

ACKNOWLEDGEMENTS

Many, many fans, collectors and researchers plus writers, artist's and publisher's have helped to garner the information used in this publication, a more complete listing of these can be found in Steve Holland's *The Mushroom Jungle - a history of Postwar Paperback Publishing*.

For established gangster-collecting fans the tremendous efforts of Steve Holland must be well-known in this field. Over many years Philip Harbottle has researched the story of post-war Science Fiction publishing and in so-doing also much on Gangsters, Westerns and other genres. This work culminated in two eponymous books coauthored with Steve Holland, *Vultures of the Void* and *British Science Fiction Paperbacks and Magazines, 1949-1956*.

Steve Chibnall, collector and researcher has made tremendous contributions, as has Thomas Lesser, collector par extraordinaire. Simon Marsh-Devine has carried out much research on artist's of the period and countless collectors and fans have contributed information, gleefully accepted by *Paperbacks, Pulps and Comics, Paperback Parade* and other fan magazines. Gary Lovisi, prolific publisher, has for many years provided an outlet, via *Paperback Parade*, for the information gathered by Steve, Phil and many others. More than this, Gary's Gryphon Publications has just began to reprint British Ace Capellis and the like for the first time in almost fifty years, so that these scarce works can be read by a new "pulp" audience.

PREFACE

This book was initially to be just a catalogue of paperbacks for sale, very scarce paperbacks that is, but it outgrew its roots almost from the outset. For the gangster books contained can certainly be classed as an endangered species, they either exist in very small numbers or in some cases may not exist at all! Surprising, considering the often large print runs they enjoyed.

The reasons for their demise were many and are as intriguing as was their postwar rise in popularity. Some of these reasons will be found in the pages before you, but more can also be found in *The Mushroom Jungle*. Some were destroyed, as a result of Police seizures (and folk tales talk of caches to be found in Police owned properties) and many had covers ripped off (as schoolboys wished to read, but not be discovered with such "pornographic" imagery). Their salacious nature meant they were never seen as literature like their contemporary paperback "Penguin" brethren. Readers were not inclined to give *White Slaves of the Congo* or *Trading With Bodies* pride of place on the mantelpiece or bookshelf. They were avidly read, and often like Westerns, passed on many times until they became so bedraggled they were fit only for the bin. So today rare items with Reginald Heade covers command a premium and collectors search for such an advertised item as Hank Janson's *Perfumed Nemesis*, that was never printed, or was It?

RESTLESS PREDATORS

Murder has always been a restless predator. In October 1944, even at the height of War when death was only a telegram away from most families, the body of taxi driver George Heath was discovered in Staines, Middlesex. Heath had been shot by Karl Hulten, a deserter from the US Army who had been seen around Hammersmith for some weeks. Some locals had nicknamed him "Chicago Joe" because he had boasted about his involvement with Chicago's gangsters; they knew he carried a loaded revolver; they knew he'd been stepping out with a local blonde. Hulten was a confident braggart and had kept Heath's Ford V8 after killing him. It was spotted within days by a patrolling constable, and Hulten found himself in a cell at Hammersmith Police Station.

The case became known as "The Cleft Chin Murder" in the tabloids of the day, and its relevant here because it was so untypical of what was then considered to be the English way of murder: with obvious exceptions, the English murder was a middle-class act of domestic-dispatching, well planned and solved only by careful investigation. Poison was the weapon of choice.

Not so with Karl Hulten and his blonde girlfriend, Elizabeth "Betty" Jones. After a failed marriage, ex-waitress Betty had worked in a series of night clubs under the name Georgina Grayson, describing herself as a strip-tease artist, which pleased the papers although it is more correct to say she was a failed strip-tease artist having only given one unsuccessful performance. She had met the tall, handsome Hulten, then calling himself Captain Ricky Rafeld, at the Hammersmith Palais. Fired up by Hulten's lies about being a big-time hood, Betty declared that she wanted to live danger- ously, "like being a gun-moll". Over the next six days, she lived her fantasy through a series of petty and not-so-petty crimes, ending with the murder of cleft-chinned taxi driver Heath.

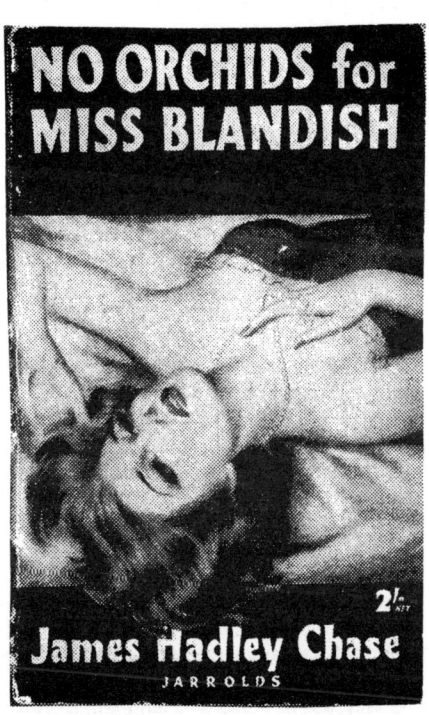

In court, she said in a half-whisper, "He told me he was a gunman, a gunman from Chicago, the leader of a gang..." In a stolen Army truck on the road between London and Reading, 18- year-old Betty decided she wanted to be a gangsters moll. A curious expression that, conjuring up images of hard-boiled private-eye yarns that you might not expect an 18-year-old girl to read. Or perhaps you might. Consider this:

A young girl comes into a shop to sell an armful of second-hand books. Amongst them is a copy of No Orchids for Miss Blandish. She smiles rather shamefacedly at the assistant. "It doesn't matter about that one if you don't want it she said nervously. Maybe we don't want it answers the assistant, but if you are not doing anything tomorrow morning come round here and watch the queue for it ... there will be one."

Although books like No Orchids were written for a male audience, women made up the majority of the customers of tuppenny libraries which were the main outlet for such books at the time. Originally published at 7s 6d in May 1939, Jarrolds reprinted in hardcover a number of times (1940, 1942, 1947) to keep up with the library demand, and issued the book as a 1/- paperback in August 1940. It was the latter edition that was picked up by the mobile male population - young, working class and lower-middle class men clutching their call up papers and often far away from home.

The market has never really reached a fork in the road. There has always been an overwhelming majority of women readers for romances, whether they were tuppenny mill-girl novelettes in the 1920s or Jaqueline Susann, who began to out-Robbins Harold Robbins in the 1960s. The bestsellers of the seventies (by the likes of Arthur Hailey and Jackie Collins) and even the bestsellers of today (by, say, John Grisham and Tom Clancy) only sell in such great numbers because they can attract both sexes. The tuppenny library readers of James Hadley Chase helped push sales of the book towards a half million copies sales figure within the first year. The truth of the matter is that women have always been attracted to bloody murder.

No Orchids for Miss Blandish was written over six weekends during the summer of 1938; at the time its author, James Hadley Chase (the pseudonym of Rene Lodge Brabazon Raymond, 1906-1985), was working as a bookseller for the wholesalers Simpkin Marshall, handling distribution to retail outlets and the tuppenny lending libraries. Writing a hard-boiled novel was purely marketing on behalf of its author, who had seen how quickly copies of *The Postman Always Rings Twice* by James M. Cain were sold; the demand for American crime thrillers was beginning to make inroads into the market of the traditional English mystery already, so much so that by 1944, even an 18-year-old ex-waitress could be seduced by the glamour of Chicago mobsters, gangs, guns and murder.

* * *

The American hard-boiled novel was heavily established in Britain by the outbreak of the War in 1939. James M. Cain's *The Postman Always Rings Twice* was first published by Jonathan Cape in 1934, with *Serenade* following in 1938; these were probably the two most influential books on the writings of Hank Janson (Stephen Frances, 1917-1989), who - along with James Hadley Chase and Peter Cheyney - was probably the most influential writer of Britain's hard-boiled school. The Cain influence on Janson was in every book, not least *Accused* which was a dramatic and simplified retelling of *Postman*. Many of Frances' stories were told in retrospect from the death cell (and often end with the accused being led away to the chair) and populated with unlikable depression-era Americans; Cain's *Serenade* offers the archetypal Janson opening with the arrival of a woman who will play an important part both criminally and emotionally in Janson's future; they erupt into violence as casually as you might change into your slip-

THE POSTMAN ALWAYS RINGS TWICE

Pocket Book 443

COMPLETE AND UNABRIDGED

4

pers. There are bits of *Double Indemnity* and *Past All Dishonour* in Janson - but then there's a lot of *Postman* in Cain's own *Galatea*.

Frances at least leapt straight into the hard-boiled mould of Cain and Horace McCoy (whose *No Pockets in a Shroud* was published in Britain in 1937) without that interim period of what might be called country noir that many British writers tried: the English mystery with its amateur detectives and inept, bumbling Scotland Yard detectives with a harder edge of Hollywood dialogue. Guns blazing in Kensington failed to make the grade with an audience who were already acquainted with the seedier alleys of L.A. via remainder copies of *Black Mask* available in Woolworths, shipped over as ballast in empty cargo ships during the 1930s. As the ballast tended to be remainder copies and the supply patchy, fans could always uncross their fingers and read Dashiell Hammett's full-length novels: *Red Harvest, The Dain Curse, The Maltese Falcon, The Glass Key and The Thin Man*, all published by Knopf between 1929-34, or Carroll John Daly's Race Williams novels, published in Britain by Hutchinsons throughout the 1930s. Daly's characters, living in the twilight zone between the law and criminal, dispensed justice with a bullet, accomplished their aims with aggression - and in so doing set up the basic tenets of hard-boiled writing.

Thus the influx of hard-boiled writers, from Daly's Race Williams novel *The Snarl of the Beast* in 1928 and W.R. Burnett's *Little Caesar* in 1929, predated the arrival of Raymond Chandler - usually envisaged by fans as the father of the British gangster paperback - by more than a decade. When *The Big Sleep* debuted from Hamish Hamilton in March 1939 it pipped James Hadley Chase's *No Orchids for Miss Blandish* by a mere two months; as Britain entered the blackout, the best-sellers included Peter Cheyney, whose American G-Man, Lemmy Caution, had first appeared in 1936 in *This Man is Dangerous*, a title echoed again and again in the fifties pulp paperback boom (*This Woman is Death* by Janson, *This Man is Death* by Ace Capelli, *This Dame Spells Death* by Chris Wheatley, etc.). Cheyney's first-person narrative was much copied, as was the

5

ersatz American slang that owed as much to Cheyney's ripe imagination as it did to dialogue he overheard around the less reputable West End dives he haunted in the name of research. Although Cheyney's Caution and Slim Callaghan stories have been damned for their violence (in Julian Symon's *Bloody Murder*, for example) they cannot be ignored. Fast moving and full-blooded, Cheyney knew what his audience wanted, and sales of 2 1/2 million a year attested to the fact that he delivered.

The influence was immediately felt. Distributors noted the arrival of more and more hard-boiled yarns: George Harmon Coxe, Frank Gruber and others from the *Black Mask* school (Coxe's *Boston Courier-Herald* photographer, Kent Murdock beating Gruber's Johnny Fletcher and Sam Cragg into the UK by five years) began to appear; British newcomers like Darcy Glinto (Harold Ernest Kelly, 1899-1969) were dog-heeling their footsteps. These new writers were treading still relatively virgin territory for British writers, but had the advantage that the American originals so influential on the hard-boiled style - the pulps - were no longer as widely available thanks to wartime import restrictions. It also meant that the early British writers - Janson, Glinto, and Ben Sarto (F. Dubrez Fawcett, 1891-1968) amongst them - culled their styles from a wider range of sources, from Cain and McCoy to Damon Runyon as well as Hollywood's gangster movies with Edward G. Robinson and Jimmy Cagney. *Little Caesar, Scarface* (said to be based on Al Capone) and *Public Enemy* (for which Cagney may have based his character on Little Hymie Weiss) lay the foundations for the gangster movie boom in the 1930s, capitalised by Hollywood in the 1940s with Laurence Tierney's portrayal of *Dillinger* and other biographical melodramas - *Al Capone, The Legs Diamond Story*, etc. The hard-boiled private eye finally made it to the screen in John Huston's 1941 classic adaptation of Hammett's *The Maltese Falcon*. Bogart became the personification of the shamus, a tough guy even without a gun as a mouthpiece; his portrayal of Philip Marlowe in *The Big Sleep* had just the right amount of contempt without losing that hint of humour, just the right amount of cruelty without losing his humanity.

This Pandoras Box of influences and the high sales figures attached to the emerging gangster paperbacks coincided with a new generation of publishers eager to supply the public with original novels (if, that is, the wartime and post-war paper supply allowed). The mushroom (or pirate) publishers, as they were dubbed, promoted their wares as blatantly as they could: Janson was "The Best of Tough Gangster Writers" (for once, the blurb was arguably right), Ben Sarto's spine-chillers were soon advertising five million sales, and other publishers were drafting their regular authors in and creating names which supposedly and instantaneously dubbed the writer a tough-as-nuts yank crimefighter: Hyman Zore, Hans Vogel, Nat Karta, Al Bocca, Duke Linton, Nick Perrelli, Hans Lugar...

Over in the States, writers like James M. Cain were actively trying to disassociate themselves from the pigeonholes they found themselves in: "I belong to no school, hard-boiled or otherwise," he wrote in his preface to *The Butterfly* (1946). The gangster and private eye novels always contained a well-documented (by critics) list of objectionable (to the critics) behaviour. Even the most literary of hard-boiled writers, Raymond Chandler, found himself at the blunt end of critical attention, writing shortly after the publication of *The Big Sleep*:

"I have only seen four notices, but two of them seemed more occupied with the depravity and unpleasantness of the book than with anything else... I do not want to write depraved books. I was aware that this yarn had some fairly unpleasant citizens in it, but my fiction was learned in a tough school and I probably didn't notice them much. I was more intrigued by a situation where the mystery is solved more by the exposition and understanding of a single character, always well in evidence, than by the slow and sometimes long-winded concatenation of circumstances. That's a point which may not interest reviewers of first novels, but it interested me very much."

If Chandlers intentions were missed by some of his reviewers, those of James Hadley Chase were bludgeoned out of existence. Criticism of Chase became a catalogue of brutality:

Guys rubbed out: 22 (with a rod, 9; with a tommy-gun, 6; with a knife, 3; with a blackjack, 2; by kicking, 1; by suicide, 1) Guys slugged bad: 16 (in the face or head, 15; in the guts, 1) Guys given a work-over: 5 (with blunt instruments, 3; with a knife, 1; with burning cigarettes, 1) Dames laid: 5 (willing, 3; paid, 1; raped, 1)

Thus critic John Mair summed up *No Orchids* in 1939. It wasn't long before the courts took notice and fined both Chase and Darcy Glinto for obscenity. But for every notice complaining of violence, the publishers noted the sales figures and demanded more of the same. It was the essence of supply and demand. Small paperback outfits could run off 25,000 copies of a gangster novel and sell it over the phone to newsagents hungry for more. The eras bestsellers - Janson, Ben Sarto, Griff - were turned out at high speed, usually one a month, and with sales of individual titles in the 40,000 plus

By the Author of "Serenade"

the Butterfly

JAMES M. CAIN

SIGNET BOOKS
Complete and Unabridged

region, a single by-line could rack up a half million sales a year. With cover prices usually between 1/6 and 2/6, a 50,000 (about $12,400 in 1948) income from one author wasn't impossible. Allowing for inflation, that's about 940,000 ($580,000) today. With costs kept to a minimum, its little wonder that these minor publishers themselves became restless predators, voracious buyers of black market paper, buying up liquidated companies for their paper allowance, and floating new companies regularly. The publishers became a complex network of producers, distributors and printers; the attrition rate in the early days was extremely high and only the ruthless survived, adapting to the changing marketplace as the austere post-war forties and early fifties clawed their way towards affluence.

* * *

It is only now, fifty years later, that these books have found themselves a toehold with a new generation. Collecting paperbacks is a slowly evolving hobby in Britain; although already well established in America, it is only in the last decade that British collectors have learned of each other. It is no longer a lonely vigil, long hours spent wandering through street markets, tramping through book fairs, boot sales and the local church jumble sale in search of tattered copies of books with titles like *Pardon My Pistol* and *Floosie on the Run*, restless predators in search of our quarry.

Around 1991, the paperback market was established well enough to host its own Paperback Fair in London, a now annual event which attracts buyers and sellers from all over the country (and one or two other countries). Dealers and collectors have established strong ties; popular areas of collecting are emerging like tributaries from the torrent of publishers and titles available; in 1993, Maurice Flanagan's Zeon Books produced my history of British postwar paperback publishing *The Mushroom Jungle*, and (thankfully) received better notices in the papers than most of the books it discussed.

Since its publication, post-Tarantino academics have discovered pulp, and authors in recent studies like *Trash Aesthetics* and *Cult Fiction* have made no bones about their vicarious enjoyment of lowbrow entertainment: Recent cultural criticism has explored more deeply than ever before the undergrowth of literature and popular film, shifting attention from what ideal audiences should be reading and viewing to what real people actually enjoy.

The academics have finally begun to realise that straightforward, down-to-earth pulp writing, which they previously only read with guilty pleasure, has as much to offer as any other form of writing. They've finally discovered what fans and collectors have known for years.

Even British gangster fiction has something to offer, as you'll find in the following pages. Not just the covers as you'll see here, although they are often reason enough. Not just the often poorly printed texts with their pidgin American slang and bouts of swinging violence, the tough-guy gang bosses and the curvaceous molls they wear on their arms, although the stories were sometimes superbly and emotionally crafted, sometimes terrible yet still charming. The publishers and the writers all had a history and life behind them which is still an unmapped; Here Be Dragons could be written starkly across them. Every book, every title, every by-line has some fascinating facet just waiting to be examined and explored. The gumshoe is on the other foot now. Now its your chance to turn detective and ask the questions. Why were these books so popular? If they were so lousy that academics ignored them for fifty years, why do so many people collect them?

Why would an 18-year-old failed stripper want to become a gangsters moll?

Read on...become a restless predator.

Steve Holland, Colchester, July 1997

ADDITION TO THE INTRODUCTION

By 1961 Panther Books, "Mushroom Publisher" survivors Hamilton & Co, reprinted *No Orchids For Miss Blandish* for a new generation. With the advent of the more enlightened 1960's, James Hadley Chase's novel was given a respectable plain front cover, no need for the glamourous seductress, having by then itself becoming part of "established" literature. The comprehensive rear cover blurb, (overlooked by the respectable looking Chase), reads as follows:

"It is no exaggeration to say that it would be difficult to find any adult person in this part of the world who had not heard of the unfortunate Miss Blandish. *No Orchids for Miss Blandish* has become the classic gangster novel and Miss Blandish a household name. The sales of the book are over two million copies. During the last war, the book was read by the men and women of the Armed Forces.

No Orchids for Miss Blandish was written in six week-ends during the late summer of 1938. It was the author's first book. It was rejected by Michael Joseph and later published in 1939 by Jarrolds Publishers(London) Ltd. An immediate success, it was quickly published in America, France, Germany, Spain, Norway, Sweden, Denmark, Finland, South America, Canada, Japan and Russia.

A WORLD BEST-SELLER

NO ORCHIDS FOR MISS BLANDISH

James Hadley Chase

over two million copies sold

In 1942 the play of the book, written by the author and Robert Nesbitt with additional dialogue by Val Guest, was presented by George Black at the Prince of Wales Theatre, London, where it ran for several months. The principle players were Robert Newton, Linden Travers, Hartley Power and Mary Clare. The provincial tour ran from 1942 to 1949. In 1945 Renown Film Company presented the film version of the book at the Plaza Cinema, London, with Linden Travers and Jack La Rue in the star roles.

No Orchids for Miss Blandish has been the subject of two studies: one by the late George Orwell called *Raffles and Miss Blandish* (Horizon, October 1944) and the other by D. Streatfield called *Persephone* (Routledge & Kegan Paul, 1959).

The present Panther edition has been re-written and revised by the author who feels the original text with its outmoded dialogue and its 1938 atmosphere would not be acceptable to the new generation of readers who may be curious to read the most controversial, the most discussed and the best known gangster story ever to have been written."

Maurice Flanagan, Westbury, England, 1997

The "alleged" secret activities of the Nun within the Convent walls has been exploited for hundreds of years. The first prosecution for obscene libel was against Edward Curll who published Venus in the Cloister or the Nun in Her Smock in 1724, and this case set the precedent for the prosecution of the "mushroom" publishers of the 1950s.

One of the favourite sexploitation texts of the postwar publishers was **the Awful Disclosures of Maria Monk**, billed as "What I Have Written is True" ..... "the Hidden Secret of Nuns Life in the Convent Exposed".

Examples amongst many are those shown her, in order:

Camden Publishing Co Ltd, 323 Upper St, Islington, N1, vg, **£5**

Pembertons, Manchester, g+, **£5**

Visart, London, svg, **£5**

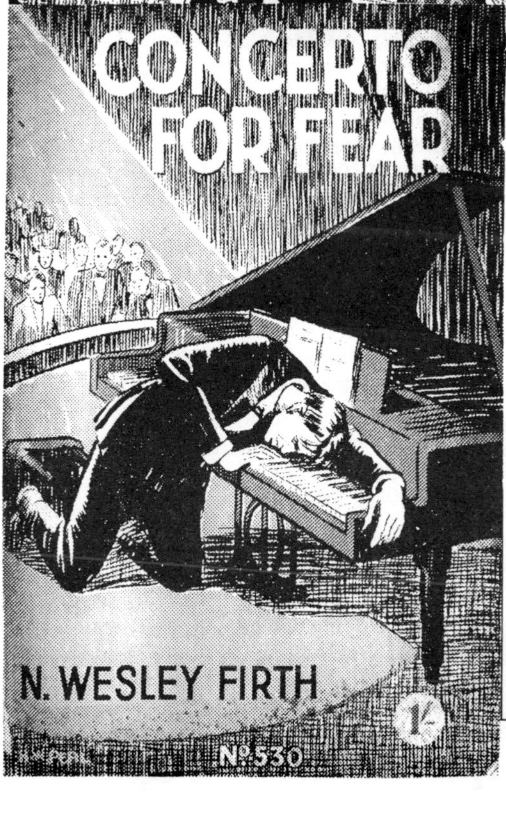

Paperbacks in the immediate post-war years were often thin flimsy publications, with one, two or three spot colour covers.

Typical of these are:

Corpses Can Walk & other stories by R Thurston Hopkins, 1946 is a 64 page oversized book from <u>Pictorial Art</u>, London with stories by Hopkins and Michael Hervey. fine **£15**

Concerto of Fear by N Wesley Firth, <u>Bear Hudson</u> (Goldhawk Rd, London, W12) #530, is a 32 page oversize booklet, 1945, cover by Perl, fine, **£15**. Bear Hudson were formed in 1943. They also published a number of Pocket Books in the same format as the US Armed Service Editions

Caravan of Crime by Elliot O'Donnell, published in 1946 by <u>Grafton Publications</u> of Dublin, the 96 pager contains ghostly crime stories from this famous ghost-hunter. vg++, **£15**

11

YOURS TRULY, HOODLUM

American writers like Hammett & Chandler, and the film spin-offs from their novels, were very influential on British popular publishing of the early 1940s. **James Hadley Chase** had written in this hardboiled style in "No Orchids For Miss Blandish" (1939) and in 1940 Harold Kelly (writing as **Darcy Glinto**) followed this style with "Lady Don't Turn Over". Both authors had works declared obscene in 1942 (a forerunner of things to come).

This Way For A Shroud by James Hadley Chase, Robert Hale, 1955, vg+, £6 ("a suspense packed thriller" involving "thugs and rackets")

Lady Don't Turn Over by Darcy Glinto, Robin Hood Press, London, 1952, vg+, £20

Yours Truly Hoodlum by Darcy Glinto, Robin Hood Press (108 Croydon Rd, London SE20, 1953, vg+ £20

CURTAINS FOR CARRIE by DARCY GLINTO

1/6

Curtains for Carrie

DARCY GLINTO

2/6

CROSS ROADS TO CRIME by FRANK WALTON

MYSTERY NOVEL

Crime Versus the LAW!

1/6

TOO LATE TO WEEP by REX RICHARDS

She wanted the bright lights
She wanted love
She got—only bitter tears

1/6

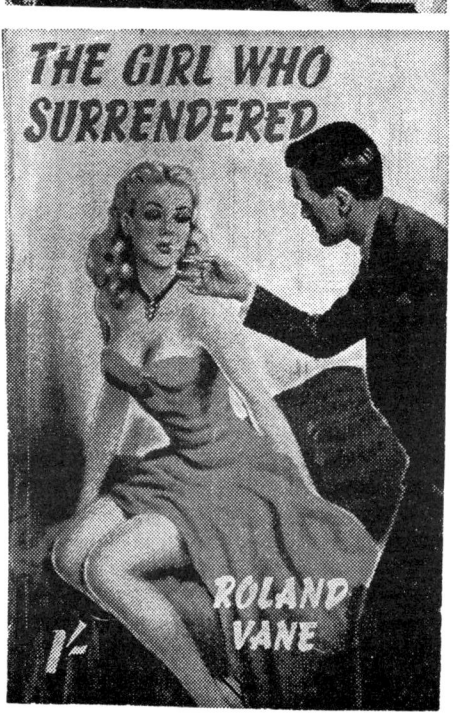

This Page:

Phoenix Press began in 1945 by reprinting Paul Renin's long-running-sexy romances. Based initially at 10 Elephant Rd, London (home of Popular Fiction (London) Ltd, they also had addresses later at Deacon St, SE17 and then 46 Kennington Place, SE11. R&L Locker distributed much of their early output.

The Auction of Souls written by survivor Aurora Mardiganian interpreted by HL Gates, (about the Great Massacre in Armenia), Perl cover?, Phoenix Press, vg-, **£10**

The Girl Who Surrendered by Roland Vane, Perl cover?, Phoenix Press, 1948, nrvg+, **£15**

Better Luck Next Crime by Michael Hervey, published by Forsyte Press (distributed by John Lever & Co, 6 Mitre St, London, EC3), nr vg, **£6.**

Like many of the paperbacks of the period, inside are ads for "Fine art Photographs of Models" from PA Leon Ltd, Harrow Rd, NW10. This was one means of advertising this riske material to a wider male audience.

Traffic in Souls by Geoffrey Pardoe, (1959 reprint (orig 1952) of the White Slavery & prostitution genre popular with the mushroom publishers). g+, **£5**

Again inside advertised are a variety of Danish Nude Studies, French Striptease etc available from the English Magazine Co., Finsbury Pavement, EC2

True Gang Life from WCM - Willam (Merritt) Publishers Ltd, 335 City Rd, EC1. vg-, **£6**

PICK-UP FOR LOVE

HENRI DUVAL

COMPLETE
6D
NOVEL

PASSION SERIES

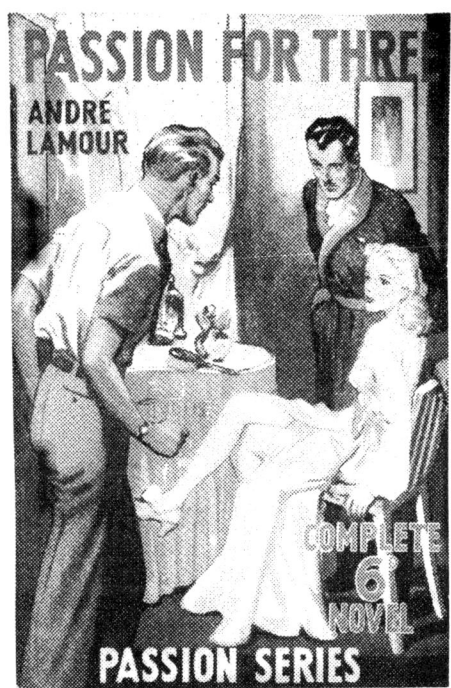

PASSION FOR THRE

ANDRÉ LAMOUR

COMPLETE
6D
NOVEL

PASSION SERIES

RUINED BY LOVE

BY
ANDRÉ LAMOUR

COMPLETE
6D
NOVEL

CRIME AND PASSION SERIES

LOVE WAS FOLLY

COMPLETE
6D
NOVEL

by
PAUL LESTRANGE

CRIME & PASSION SERIES

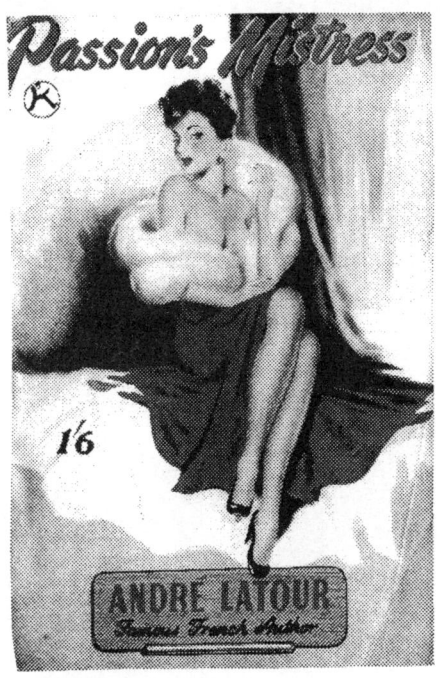

Previous page:

The sexy French romance had been popular since the late eighteenth century. **Curzon Publishing/Murray & Nichols** of Church St, Stone in Staffordshire were publishing their 31 page "Crime & Passion" and "Passion" series' in the immediate post-war years. **Clifford Lewis** was the man behind this operation using french-sounding housenames like Paul Lestrange, Henri Duval, Gaston Lamond and Andre Lamour with Earl Ellison and the genuine Wesley Firth. All available for the princely sum of six pence.

Pick-Up For Love by Henri Duval, vg+, £10

Passion For Three by Andre Lamour, vg+, £10

Ruined by Love by Andre Lamour, vg+, £10

Love Was Folly by Paul Lestrange, vg+, £10

This Page:

Kaye Publications of Southampton Row, WC1. They were one of several companies distributed by Gaywood Press. Bernard and Alfred Kaye continued the older french-romances of **Andre Latour** whilst also publishing a large number of gangster and sexploitation novels by Ace Capelli, Johnny Grecco, Josh Wingrave and others.

Passions Mistress, vg+, £15

Shameless, vg++, £20

Latour is described as a "brilliant young French writer translated for the first time" who "writes with tenderness and abandon." The last word of the blurb, the cover image and title all promise the reader sex!

Edwin Self had been around in the publishing business long enough to know that French low-life novel with alluring ladies (of dubious reputation) spelled money. With authors like George Louis Delmaine, Marc Lavelle, Michael Lesage and Jean Paul Valois exploring the byways of the Paris district of Montmartre home of the Folies Bergere and all things daring. Despite the claims for original translation, UK native Lisle Willis wrote under the Valois byline.

Valois describes the life of "artists models and midinettes, the Paris Underworld "... "a poor boy in Montmartre" and of "French Maquis imprisoned by the Gestapo" in Chere Amis.

Chere Amis by Jean-Paul Valois, fine, £15

Corinne by Jean-Paul Valois, 1953, fine, £15

Affair in Paris by Georges Louis Delmaine, fine, £15

The Leicester based **Harborough Publishing Co Ltd** was taken over by Raymond & Lillian Locker in 1948. The revamped Harborough initially published Paul Renin's racy romances and then titillating French novels (originally translated by Raymond Locker). Meanwhile their Archer Press imprint ran gangster stories from Spike Morelli, Michael Storme and Gene Ross.

My Life Is My Own by Jules-Jean Morac, 1953, vg+, **£15**, the author is a "volatile Frenchman" who "knows Montmartre and the Latin Quarter"

Life of Tilly Gourd, 1953, vg+, **£15**

Amazingly these French novels were reprinted into the 1960s by Verlock, Trident and Award Publications.

The Harem by Louis Charles Royer was first printed in 1950, then reprinted in 1952, 1953 and 1963!

Here is the 60s reprint, vg++, **£5**

Along with most of the mushroom publishers **Brown Watson** ploughed the French furrow with "original French stories" from Edwin Laforge and Charles Lefevre. The novels offered the reader "passion and fury", "glamour and good times", whatever this implied!

Modern Fiction also exposed the oldest profession, one that seemed much more acceptable if set in France. Rene Laroche was actually the prolific writer Ernest McKeag, so why the novels had to be "translated from the french" is a bit of a mystery.

Paris Model by Edwin Laforge, Brown Watson, vg+ £15

Montmartre by Charles Lefevre, Brown Watson, vg+, £15

Ladies of Leisure by Rene Laroche, 1951, cover by Pollack, svg, £10

All beautiful ladies, the latter encouraging a modern-day kerbcrawler!

Almost the only factor influencing the success or failure of the postwar publishers was access to paper. **Gerald G Swan Ltd** was able to build up stocks of titles before the war and was able to profit from these whilst still obtaining his own paper ration. Swan published comics, girls and boys stories, novels as well as detective, romance and SF paperbacks & pulps. All were cheaply produced with mainly two colour poor quality artwork (making them somewhat endearing!).

From 1939 Swan reprinted American SF stories and in 1940 produced Weird Story, then Yankee Science Fiction & Detective Fiction, later Weird Shorts, Occult Shorts and the Crime Shorts series'.

Above: **Crime Shorts #2 & #4**

Across: **Vengeance Shorts #1**

Fine booklets 36 pages and **£8 each**

21

Gerald G. Swan had offices at Edgeware House, Burne St, Marlybone. His early success was publishing over 60 novels by Paul Renin (Richard Goyne) and William J Elliot. The rights to both authors were later sold out to the developing Harborough/R&L Locker empire where Renin continued to be reprinted. Swan's natural business acumen developed as a teenage bookseller in Church Street Market meant he would happily cash in on any publishing market that developed.

The distinctive Crime Albums of the late 1940s and the blue/white covered Crime Shorts and Detective Shorts were full of "gripping yarns" and "swift moving" tales of crime, justice, peril and death.

Above: Detective Shorts #1 & #4

Across: Thrill Shorts fine at £8 each

Reginald Cyril Webb Heade (1901-1957) is one of Britain's few true masters of paperback cover art and ranks with the finest of American illustrators.

In his native Britain Heade is known for the hundreds of "menaced dame" covers he produced for "mushroom publishers" such as R&L Locker, Harborough, Archer, Gaywood Press and countless others in the late 1940s and early 1950s. The scantily clad ladies posed provocatively, whilst Heade's attention to drapery, hair, flesh tone and shadow gave him superiority amongst his contemporary commerical artists. In the USA his reputation rests on about fifty covers on Leisure Library and Kaywin/Archer paperbacks of the early 1950s.

In fact it is with these US paperbacks that British collectors can more easily find his best dame covers (for a price!), as most of his British gangster and good girl art covers are increasingly almost impossible to locate.

Heade's "Hank Janson" covers for the Gaywood/SD Frances/New Fiction publishing lines are among his more famous and collected works. His lurid covers ensured huge sales for Stephen Frances' pseudo American gangster novels, with many million sellers (claimed!), five series in digest format, leading on to the later Moring & Roberts & Vintner lesser works of the late 50s and 60s. The tales of sex and violence were much copied by other writers and publishers and led to gaol sentences for publishers Carter and Reiter in 1954 on obscenity charges.

The novels contained little to justify the prosections but undoubtedly Heade's ravished dames were deemed too dangerous for the work-

ing class male, publishers having to resort to overprinting many thousands of books with Hank Janson's silhouette colophon.

"Delicate, colourful, beautiful and erotic" are words used to describe Heade's dames of the 1947-1954 period, his women have a quality rarely produced "on the conveyor belt of commercial art". But Heade was not just a good girl art painter, his talents were much greater than this. In recognition, publishers sought his talent to paint covers for slick magazines like Brittania & Eve, juvenile hardbacks like WE Johns Worrals series and Elsie J Oxenham's Abbey Girls books besides "Perry Mason" detective novels for Cassells.

Even when the notoriety of his Hank Janson dames led to less work for the real Reginald Heade, he was able to re-invent himself as Cy Webb to produce glorious covers for Pan and Panther from 1956 to 1958. These later covers rank as some of the best of British paperback cover-artwork and only rarely is there a glimpse of the recognisable good girl to give the game away.

Over the period from 1942-1958 Heade produced a huge body of work that also included Sexton Blake Library covers and Confessions magazine cover art and Mills & Boon hardback romances, plus many comic strips. Heade covers in his "gangster" period in vg+ condition invarably sell for £30 and more.

I certainly cannot argue with Steve Chibnall's claim for Heade as "Englands Greatest Artist" made in the seminal monograph about Heade published by Books Are Everything (RC Holland) in 1991.

Previous page:

Tension #39 in sequence of Hank Janson novels (4th series), claiming sales of 3 million - one assumes for the whole series to date!

svg-vg+ condition £30

This Dame Dies Soon in vg+ condition, an earlier book claiming only one million sales

£30

Above:

Sadie Don't Cry Now by Hank Janson "best of the tough gangster authors", #34 in sequence (3rd series)

vg+ condition at £30

kill her' if you can

2/-

HANK JANSON

AUTHOR of BEST SELLING GANGSTER STORIES

Conflict

2/-

HANK JANSON

(THREE MILLION SALE)

Vengeance

2/-

HANK JANSON

FIVE MILLIONS SALE

Suspense

2/-

HANK JANSON

THREE MILLION SALE

Previous Page:

Kill Her If You Can #36 (3rd series). vg+ condition **£30**

Conflict #38 . Light cover crease about vg+ **£30**

Vengeance #45. Cover etc vg+ but about 1/2 ins off spine. **£30**

This Page:

Pursuit #44 (4th series) nrvg+ **£30**

Torment #47 (4th series). Great bondage cover. svg **£30**

Silken Menace #50 (5th series). vg condition but 1ins off spine. To compensate it has a full colour illustration of Perfumed Nemesis on the rear cover! **£25**

The seven books named in the original Hank Janson trial were: Accused, Killer, Pursuit, Vengeance, Amok, Auctioned and Persian Pride. The first five were part of the 4th series, the 5th was aborted.

REGINALD CYRIL WEBB HEADE

Leisure Library of New York produced a series of 23 digest sized paperbacks in 1952/3 reprinting British gangster novels by such as Roland Vane, Spike Morelli, Michael Storme. These were house-names used by R&L Locker , the novels being originally printed in Britain in 1951/2. The majority of the titles sported superb Heade covers, as do the six shown here. All are in near fine condition (a little waterstaining on rear does not detract) and are for sale at **£30** each.

#2 Death For A Doll by Spike Morelli

#3 Pick-Up Girl by Roland Vane

#4 Make Mine A Shroud by Michael Storme

Many of the original R & L Locker typically Menaced Dame covers by Heade are almost impossible to find in Britain, making the Leisure Library series most desirable to collectors.

The Locker/Harborough/Archer publishers had made the connection with US publishers. And so they completed a strange circle of the pseudo-american gangster novel written by British authors for a book-starved post-war public re-export itself to its original New York & Chicago breeding ground. What did the US male of the period make of a USA invented in downtown Blackpool or the back streets of Soho?

#6 Hot Dames on Cold Slabs by Michael Storme

#7 This Way For Hell by Spike Morelli

#8 White Slave Racket by Roland Vane. **All near fine at £30 each**

R&L Locker was the publishing house started by husband and wife team Raymond and Lilian Locker . From their base at Hanley, near Stoke-on-Trent they began by publishing childrens comics and hardback romances. In 1948 they took over Harborough Publishing and founded Archer Press. The long running Paul Renin byline together with the likes of Pierre Flammeche were often coupled with enticing Heade artwork (at his best) to encourage large sales. In January 1954 all the Locker companies ceased trading. Many of the Locker/ Archer titles were exported to the USA or republished by Kaywin of Cleveland, Ohio in 1951.

It was only recently that Locker/ Heade artwork emerged at auction.

The books are extremely rare in the UK and it is often in only the American editions that nice copies can be found.

Previous Page:

Outrage by Paul Renin vg+ condition £25

Men Women Love about vg+ £25

Atonement vg- condition but rare £20

The Renin/Heade's were well painted but more subdued than much of Heade's art of the period, reflecting the less lurid nature of this romance byline (nevertheless implying sexual impropriety or illicit love of a less salacious nature). All were published in 1949.

This Page:

Sinful Sisters by Roland Vane fine £35

Flame by Paul Renin fine £30

Vice Rackets of Soho by Roland Vane fine £50

All were published by Kaywin in 1951 (originally Archer novels in UK).

Leisure Library replaced Kaywin publishers in reprinting Archer and Harborough books in 1952. 24 titles later and in just the following year the New York operation closed down (the Lockers having returned to England in June 1952).

These US editions were in digest size and featured gangster authors like Michael Storme, Spike Morelli, Gene Ross besides the romance and sexploitation of Paul Renin, Roland Vane and Jules-Jean Morac.

My Life Is My Own by Jules-Jean Morac, cover by David Wright, 1952, Leisure Lib #1, vg+, £10

No Prude by Jules-Jean Morac, cover by David Wright, 1952, some watermarking on rear cover otherwise, Leisure Lib #6, vg+, £10

Amorous Adventuress by Roland Vane, cover by Heade, 1952, Leisure Lib #16, vg, £15

Rare **Heade** covers on this page are **Dark Waterfront** by Michael Hervey, Hamilton, 1947, vg-, **£20**

One of just a few he did for this publisher (artists more frequently used by Hamiltons include Perl and Oliver Brabbins).

Reginald Heade and David Wright were the principal cover illustrators for the Lockers' Harborough imprint.

Harborough Publishing Co Ltd survived between 1950 and 1953 operating out of 20-22 Vine Street, Hanley, Stoke-on-Trent.

Demon of Desire by William J Elliot, Heade cover, Harborough, 1950, vg+, **£30**

Lost Souls in Bohemia by William J Elliot, Heade cover, Harborough, 1951, vg-, **£5.**

Who would spoil a Heade cover by inking around the ladies boobs!

Amongst the best of Reginald Heade's covers for the Locker empire were the **Michael Storme** books. These consisted of eleven Storme's for The Archer Press between 1949 and 1950 (three covers by Heade, one by Thorpe and the remainder by Pollack) and fourteen Stormes for Harborough Publishing (all with Heade covers) in the period 1952-5.

The success of George Dawson's (Michael Storme) "uncompromising" Private Eye, Nick Cranley, in no short measure due to the excellent artwork used on the books. Dawson also wrote as Nick Perrelli for his own company, Tempest Publications.

Satan Buys A Wreath, The Archer Press, 1951, nrfine, £35

Elvira Digs A Grave, Harborough Publishing, 1952, nrfine, £35

One Man in His Time by Hank Janson (Frances - autobiographical), Gaywood Press, Heade, vg+, £20

Overleaf: Four of the seven Hank Janson titles cited at the Old Bailey in 1954 as obscene libels (and subject to destruction orders). All were published by New Fiction Press and distributed by Gaywood Press Ltd. in 1952.

Accused, Heade cover, vg+ £35

Auctioned, near vg+, £25

Killer, Heade cover, vg+, £35

Persian Pride, vg+, £25

The other books involved in the case were *Amok*, *Vengeance* and *Pursuit*.

This page: New Fiction/Top Fiction

Murder, 1952, Heade, vg+, £35

Desert Fury, 1952, Heade, svg, £30

Nyloned Avenger, 1953, Heade cover, (*Silken Menace* - Heade cover on rear), vg+, £35

Also advertised but never to appear were *Woman Trap*, *Perfumed Nemesis*, *Blonde Dupe* & *Britains Great Flood Disaster*.

The byline of <u>Roland Vane</u> was originally used in the late 1920s on a series of sexy novels published by Gramol. This pseudonym and others like Paul Reville and Henri Lamonte continued to be used on postwar paperbacks to cash in on their salacoius pre-war reputation. French sounding titles or authors hinted, that possibly between these pages, the boundaries of good taste prevailing at the time would be crossed.

Examples here are R&L Locker titles reprinted by Kaywin in the USA in 1951.

White Slaves of New Orleans is the 1951 reprint (Cover with green dress), painted by Heade vg+ condition £30

Ladies of the Red Lamp (1951), Heade cover. Near fine (slight stain on rear) £30

Night Haunts of Paris (1951) artist unknown. Fine £20

The pseudonym <u>Paul Renin</u> was to be used on scores of paperbacks over five decades from the 1920's to the 1960's. The prolific Richard Goyne was the man behind the pen-name. The pen-name was synonymous with exciting, titillating tales of fallen women and extramarital sex. These sensational romances were guaranteed to sell in large numbers to one assumes an essentially male audience even if purporting to aim at females, the Black Lace or **Nexus** novel of the day (with only obtuse reference to the act of sex).

Love (note the pound inference), Harborough (R & L Locker) Heade cover fine £30

Weekend Wives, Archer Press, Heade cover vg- £15

Sex, (Kaywin, 1951), fine condition, artist unknown, £20

SOME GUYS DON'T DIE SOON ENOUGH
SOME DAMES DIE TOO SOON

TIPTOE THRO' A GRAVEYARD

24

MICHAEL STORME

Coffin for a Cutie

1/6

by

SPIKE MORELLI

SULTRY LOVE

LOUIS ARTHUR CUNNINGHAM

35¢

Shuna

and the LOST TRIBE

by JOHN KING

16

Some of Heade's most effective artwork graces the covers shown overleaf from the Harborough/Archer stable.

Tiptoe Thro' A Graveyard, Michael Storme (Harborough) vg+ **£35**

Coffin For A Cutie by Spike Morelli from Archer (1950) fine **£35**

Sultry Love by Louis Arthur Cunningham (Archer Press) fine **£30**

Shuna and the Lost Tribe by John King is one of Heade's most sought after covers. Not renowned for fantasy covers, the two Shunas and the Hank Janson novel "Unseen Assassin" are amongst the few that venture into the Fantasy/SF area. Shuna is a "tarzanesque" jungle girl, a genre cashed in on in the 1950s by WH Allen's Goulden & Pinnacle novels . However in this novel author Ernest McKeag crosses "lost world adventure" with space opera. Published by Harborough in 1951, 1ins off spine o/w vg+ **£35**

On this page:

Shown across are two rare covers by Heade by even more ephemeral publishers.

Some Dames Die Quick by Timothy Trenton published in 1952 by Burmont Book Distributors of 69 Elgin Ave, London, W9 vg++ **£35**

Lady, Your Gun's Showing by Timothy Trenton was published by Galliard Publications of 38 York Place, Edinburgh vg++ **£35**

There was clearly a connection between the two operations and the Trenton byline was used on other Heade/Trenton books that are equally scarce (eg. Deception), whilst Burmont produced at least two other gangsters (Illus. by Pollack)

The debauched lives of fallen women and serial seducers recounted by the likes of Pierre Flammeche, Roland Vane and Paul Renin in the 1930s-60s followed in the tradition of scandalous novels from French authors like Paul de Kock (what a name!), Emile Zola and Guy de Maupassant (often written in the nineteenth century). All were described as "realistic" with "literal" translations, and when combined with a lurid cover, seduced the reader into the belief that those normally hidden and unspoken of delights would appear in text form.

Alas other than the words bed and naked little else was revealed!

The Man With the Three Pair of Breeches published by Mathiessen in the early 1900s vg £10

Spoiled Lives by Flammeche (Heade), Kaywin, 1951 vg+ £30

Sinful Sisters by Vane (Heade), Kaywin, 1951 fine £35.

The "Confessions" type story is a hardy perennial of British publishing aimed at both female and male audiences. In the 1970s Timothy Lea and Rosie Dixon Confessions books by Futura sold millions of copies, even led to spin-off films.

Post-war Britain led the way with many ephemeral publications by "Mushroom" publishers of such amoral tales like **"Amorous Confessions Number 1"** from Rayburn Productions of 76 Farleigh Rd, London, N6. The 32 page (plus colour cover) oversized booklet features five short romance stories with a sexy cover girl by **Nat Long**. fine condition £10

Rayburn also published **Personal Confessions**, the issue above (was it the only one?) sported a Heade dame. Little known publishers Rayburn was a spin-off company from Martin & Reid (they are advertised inside). Bob Monkhouse was working for them at the time - and Rayburn was named after one of Monkhouse's friends svg copy £20

Innocent Confessions was another such pamphlet issued by Grant Hughes (an off shoot of Curtis Warren, in itself an offshoot of Hamilton & Co - in this incestuous postwar publishing world). Cover by Heade, the booklet contains three stories on of which is I Married a Gunman by Sheila J Jaxon). Cover some creasing but rare item at £20

Phantom Detective Cases is an oversized booklet featuring Earl Ellison and, the prolific, N. Wesley Firth stories. Ellison was typical gangster pseudonym whilst Firth was a real name, who was capable of churning out 6000 words a day to order in almost any genre including saucy romance, fantasy/SF, gangster and even fairy stories. He was the self-acclaimed "Prince of Pulp Peddlers". John Spencer & Co (one of the longest running of the mushroom publishers) issued this pulp-sized booklet in 1948. Sporting a great FT cover in fine condition **£10**

MAYFAIR NIGHTS

2/6

STUDIO REVELS

TWO SHILLINGS AND SIXPENCE

Little is known of the British artist **HW Perl**. On his day Perl could paint a fair beauty (without being of the class of a Heade). He turned out a large number of girlie covers for Modern Fiction, Bernardos, Curtis Warren, Hamilton, R&L Locker, Hermitage, Grant Hughes, Kaner and others in the post-war years. In Crimetime Simon Marsh-Devine claims Perl's covers are often "mannerset, typified by long limbs and often, strange, impossible poses. The face of the woman is often the only part of the picture that is well-detailed, with extremities such as hands being poorly drawn." Again as Marsh-Devine points out that publishers often got what they paid for, with payments for covers low and the need to paint many quickly to deadline, few artists were prepared to provide the quality and detail that Heade or later Pan artists Tayler or Peffer would offer. So perhaps Perl is judged too harshly, although his attempts to portray BEMs (Bug Eyed Monsters) for the pulps were often hilariously naive.

Perl's stylistic dames together with the much more stunning dames by Heade have come to characterise the artwork of gangster and romance novels of the post-war era of "mushroom" publishers and I for one can be counted as a fan.

Mayfair Nights by Henri Duval

Studio Revels by N Wesley Firth

Published by Hamilton & Co (Stafford) Ltd in the late 1940s both are near vg+ and **£15**

Hamiltons began in 1946 later producing romance, crime and SF novels plus the long running Authentic Science Fiction magazine.

Perl painted covers for a number of the "mushroom" publishers of the post war years, many signed and many unsigned (or cropped). His style is distinctive yet like earlier works are less obvious to spot.

Hamilton & Co were amongst the very early post-war publishers and it was here that Perl painted several covers.

Strange Hunger by Michael Hervey (Hamiltons, 1946) svg **£15**

Curtis Warren Ltd started in Spring 1948 as an offshoot of Hamiltons. Joseph Pacey and ex-Hamiltons editor Edwin Self set up the new company.

Miss Pinki Pays Off by Brett Vane (Curtis Warren, 1950) svg **£15**

Maria by Brett Vane (Curtis Warren, 1951) vg- **£15**

Both were out & out gangster yarns typical of the period.

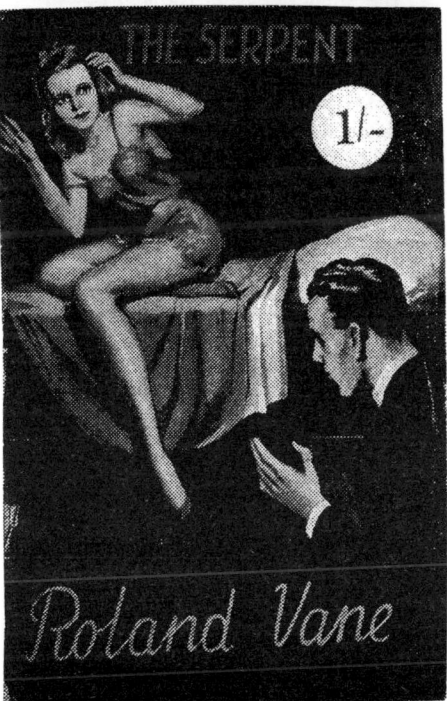

The prolific Frederick Foden was the writer behind the pseudonym **Brett Vane** as well as many other pen-names including Nick Baroni and Kirk David.

Curtis Warren in the early days would also re-use old Grant Hughes artwork (another company spawned by DA Fletcher & Joseph Pacey, directors of Hamilton & Co). Curtis initially based themselves at Grays Inn Road, London before moving to Lambs Conduit St, WC1 for the majority of their profligate output in the period 1950-1954.

Nobody's Dame by Brett Vane vg-£15

Smart Girl svg £15

Both were painted by Perl and published in 1951 by Curtis Warren

The Serpent by Roland Vane was published by Phoenix Press (1949?) and looks like a Perl cover vg £15

The small publisher **Kaner Publishing Co** of Llandudno also used Perl as cover artist for a number of crime, western and fantasy titles in the 1944-1948 period. The established writer John Russell Fearn was used on a few fantasy and westerns, but most of the output was self publishing by owner Hyman Kaner. The flimsy 80 page paperbacks together with a few more substantial hardbacks were virtually impossible to find in Britain until a number turned up in a US warehouse find. This enabled collectors to obtain often fine copies at reasonable prices. Most of this find has now been dispersed into collectors' hands.

Slaves of Ijax by John Russell Fearn (1947) fine **£5**

The Cynics Desperate Mission by Kaner nrvg+ **£15** (includes SF story)

An Alibi Too Much by Kaner vg+ **£15**

Both published in 1946

Perl was capable on his day of dramatic artwork and a fine portrayal of the female form.

The Sun Queen by H Kaner sports a fine Perl dustjacket over a hardback book , vg++/vg++, **£30**

People of the Twilight Zone is the other fantasy related hardback published by Kaner in 1946. dustjacket is vg+, **£30.**

Devils Play-ground by Roland Vane was published by Modern Fiction in 1949, vg+, **£20.**

The pseudonym **Roland Vane** was used by writer **Ernest McKeag**, (an editor with the Amalgamated Press since 1923). He was better known for his boys and girls fiction and had used the Vane by-line since the 1920s.

Roland Vane was to sell millions of books for Phoenix, Archer Press and Modern Fiction in the postwar years.

HW Perl's covers combined with Frank Dubrez Fawcett's tough gangland stories as Ben Sarto guaranteed huge sales for the postwar publishers. Sarto alone was said to have garnered sales of 5-6 million.

Fawcett was born in Great Drifield in 1891. He served in the Great War and his first novel was published in 1923 as H. Dupres. The novel was typical of the risque romance popular since the days that pulp paperbacks rolled off the presses in the nineteenth century. His publishers were Mowl and Gray, later to be Gramol, the forerunners of the postwar mushroom publishers.

The Sarto novels dug dirt from slavery, illegal hootch rackets, dope dealing and gangsterism set against skylines as far apart as New York and Soho.

Fawcett and Modern Fiction Ltd teamed up from the latter's outset in 1945, with two 32 page novelettes by Eugene Glen, another alter-ego of Fawcett. Fawcett penned scores of tough Sarto's for Modern Fiction (and for Hermitage Publications), often at a rate of one a month. Eddie Turvey, founder of Modern Fiction had struck the mother lode with Sarto, and the formula would be copied by other less long-lived publishers. Fawcett also wrote Sarto's for Milestone, concentrating here on the revelations of Miss Otis (Miss Otis Blows Town, Plays Ball etc).

Well over a hundred novels and a timespan from 1946 to 1958, Miss Otis and Ben did blow town for the last time and Modern Fiction soldiered on until 1961 before they too expired.

I'll Kill 'Em Inch By Inch, 1949, Modern Fiction, Perl cover, vg+, £20

Chicago Dames, 1947?, Modern Fiction, Perl Cover, vg++, £20

EH Turvey's empire grew, not only in publishing, but also in printing and distribution. Risque French style novels by **Raymond Lacroix** were published by offshoot **Bernardo Amalgamated Industries Ltd,** (distributed by Modern Fiction). They were just 64 pages in length and claimed to be "printed on Good Quality paper", (times were hard!), and "the finest value in light literature". Turvey continued to use Perl cover art for these and other Modern Fiction authors like Raymond Buxton and the indefatigable Roland Vane (Ernest McKeag).

Romantic Moments, 1948, vg+, £15

Love's Tempest, 1948, creased cover, o/wise vg+ £10

Love Finds A Way, vg+, £15

The latter novel claims "All film and dramatic rights reserved". An option, as far as I am aware, not taken up by Hollywood or even Pinewood.

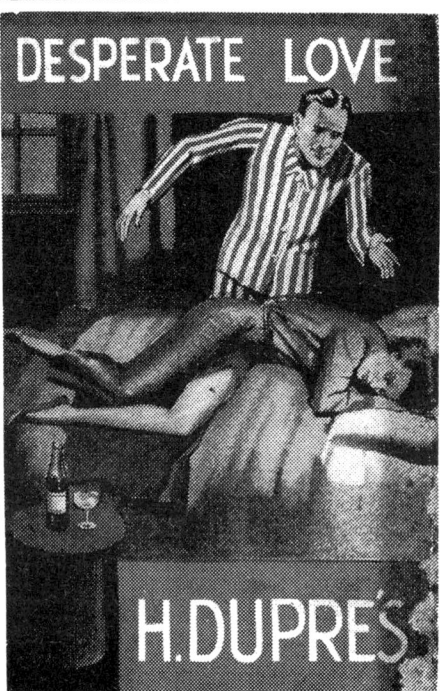

13 FRENCH STREET

GIL BREWER

HANK JANSON says READ THIS BOOK!

25 CENTS

2/-

AN ORIGINAL AMERICAN NOVEL - NOT A REPRINT

Satan Is a Woman

GIL BREWER

HANK JANSON says READ THIS BOOK!

25 CENTS

2/-

AN ORIGINAL AMERICAN NOVEL NOT A REPRINT

Forever Francy

ZORE REACHES NEW HEIGHTS WITH AN AMERICAN EPIC THAT SHATTERS EVERY ILLUSION

1/6

HYMAN ZORÉ

HANS VOGEL

As never before a powerful novel of America's gangland told with fearless conviction!

1/6

Main Drag

Ben Sarto detailed Miss Otis' escapades and the inside story on New York's sleazy underworld for Modern Fiction, Knole Park Press, Beacon and Milestone between 1946 and 1958, amassing huge sales (and financial rewards) for the publishers.

Manhattan Terrors, Modern Fiction, 1952, g++, £8

Miss Otis Episode 8, Milestone, 1954, g+, £5

Miss Otis Episode 9, Milestone, 1954, g++, £5

By 1954 the Vice Squad had got its teeth into the purveyors of "pornographic" gangster novels and Frank Fawcett dropped from the scene to write for a more "respectable" market. Modern Fiction came under the scrutiny of the courts for titles like "Trading With Bodies" (a Griff white slavery novel) whilst Alistair Paterson and others continued the Sarto line for a further four years.

ESPIONAGE

BEN SARTO

A HOUSE OF TERROR...

2/-

"HERE COMES THE BRIBE"

BLAIR JOHNS

2/-

DARCY GLINTO
Introduces

ORDEAL BY SHAME

2/-

by SARAH PRENTISS

A Guy Must Live

JOHNNY DARK

MILESTONE 2/- BOOKS
U.K.

EXTORTION INCORPORATED

BY JOHN COOPER 1/6

A WORLD DISTRIBUTORS NOVEL

NO PROFIT IN MURDER

BY CARL JOHNSON 1/6

A WORLD DISTRIBUTORS NOVEL

murdered girl — a wrongly accused man — and!

THE HOUR OF JUSTICE

by Richard Milne

Previous Page:

Espionage by Ben Sarto, Modern Fiction, 1957, Ray Theobald cover, g+, £6

"Here Comes The Bribe" by Blair Johns, Modern Fiction, 1954, Ray Theobald cover, vg, £8

Ordeal by Shame by Sarah Prentiss (Introduced by Darcy Glinto), risque abortion story, Robin Hood Press, 1951, vg++, £10

A Guy Must Live by Johnny Dark, Milestone, 1954, g++, £6

This Page: World Distributors

Extortion Incorporated by John Cooper, 1951, g++, £8

No Profit in Murder by Carl Johnson, 1951, nrvg+, £12

The Hour of Justice by Richard Milne, WDL All Star Detective No126, 1954, g+, £5

World Distributors published in Manchester, England and also in Canada in collaboration with Sydney Pemberton (a publisher of romance, thriller and westerns since 1941). One of their most popular authors was Dale Bogard described as "the fastest thriller writer on Earth". Douglas Enefer was a Mancunian and wrote as Bogard and then later under his own name for the 1960s Consul TV tie-in The Avengers. WDL were survivors from the Mushroom period publishing conventional paperbacks as WDL, Viking and Consul.

Nine Times Dead by Dale Bogard, 1951, vg-, £6

Nobody Died For Johnnie by Dale Bogard, 1951, vg, £8

Careless Virgin by James Clayford, nrvg+, £15 - this reprints the US digest Astro Books #17, cover by Rodewald.

World Distributors were not the only "mushroom" publishers in the North West.

Jasmit Publications of Grimshaw St, Burnley published gangsters by Gordon Shayne (And So to Death is billed as the 69th exclusive Shayne story). Jasmit like several other small publishers "tried" gangsters alongside their "joke" and "gag" books. Publishers may have been chased for these novels by the law, but (often attracting less public attention) they published girly photographic books, that I suspect generated more profit.)

And So To Death by Gordon Shayne, Denis McLoughlin cover (whilst moonlighting from TV Boardman), Jasmit, 1952, abt vg, **£20**

Floosie on the Run by Slim Vincent, 1950, World Dist, vg, **£10**

Front Page Murder by John Powers, All Star WDL #139, svg, **£9**

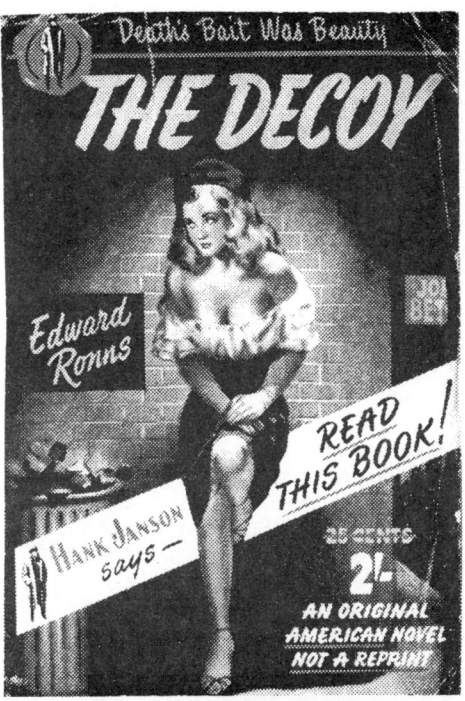

Gaywood Distributors Ltd was launched in 1947 by Julius Reiter. Reiter was opposed to the Nazis and left his native Germany for England in 1933. He built up Kosmos International Agency, publishing newspapers, magazines and books. During the war he was interned on the Isle of White and then Canada and returned to England after the War.

In 1948 Gaywood began to distribute Hank Janson. In 1951 Reiter started publishing Hank Janson under his New Fiction Press imprint. With Janson's great success, Reiter began to reprint "real hard-boiled" US authors like Edward Ronns and Gil Brewer (on Janson's recommendation!)

The Decoy by Edward Ronns, New Fiction, 1952, nrvg+, **£15**

I Can't Stop Running by Ronns, New Fiction, 1952, vg+, **£15**

So Rich, So Dead by Gil Brewer, Gaywood, 1952, vg+, **£20**

One of the most prolific of the "mushroom" publishers was **Scion Ltd**. The main mover behind Scion was BZ Immanuel, A Latvian born in Riga in 1907. He came to Britain as a pauper in the escape from Hitler's Europe and decided to stay. In 1947 Scion issued a photo booklet featuring Rita Hayworth, this was an immediate success for the fledgling publisher. In 1948 Immanuel branched out to publish a series of comics (Big Time, Big Shot etc.), using Ron Embleton & Ron Turner (used to great effect as cover artist for the Vargo Statten novels of the 50s) as artists. Also in 1948 the first of a several series of romance novelettes were issued. By the 1950s Scion was the third largest of the mushroom publishers, behind Curtis Warren and Hamilton & Co.

Scion quickly discovered the lucrative gangster, western and sci-fi markets. Authors like Norman Firth, Stephen Frances (as Duke Linton), Bevis Winter, Donald Cresswell, Vic Hansen, Michael Barnes and Dail Ambler wrote under a plethora of american sounding pen-names like Duke Linton, Brad Shannon, Ricky Drayton, Danny Spade and many others. In 1952 and then again in 1954 they were fined for publishing "pornographic" gangster stories, this became their death knell.

The house-name Duke Linton was used by Steve Frances (of Hank Janson fame), Frank Dubrez-Fawcett, Vic Hansen and Norman Lazenby.

Crazy To Kill, published in 1950, Ferrari cover, vg+ **£15**

Killer Bait, Scion #510/3/53 published 1953, cover by Roger Davis, vg **£10**

60

LET'S SHOOT THIS OUT

Ross Angel

1/6

YOU DON'T DIE TWICE

1/6

BY ROSS ANGEL

A SCION AMERICAN THRILLER

1/3

AMERICAN THRILLER 1/6

Dames Dont Dictate

A ROSS ANGEL Thriller

No percentage in Death

ROSS ANGEL

SCION AMERICAN THRILLER

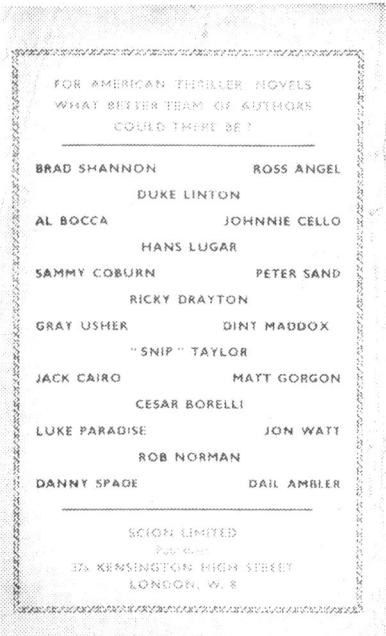

Donald Cresswell wrote a number of gangster novels for Scion under the pen-name of **Ross Angel**. Angel "has made a special study of crime among the young hoods, the killers, the hop-heads, and the young women they consort with..."

Let's Shoot This Out, 1951, Ferrari cover, svg, **£15**

You Don't Die Twice, 1952, vg, **£15**

Dames Don't Dictate, #43499, 1952, vg+, **£20**

No Percentage In Death, nrvg+, 1953, **£15**

This page:

Give Me A Gun, 1952, vg, **£15,** rear cover shows Scion's 20 big name gangster writers.

Johnny Cello is a name used by Vic Hansen, Michael Barnes & others.

Light Out!, #47399, Roger Davis cover, vg+, **£20**

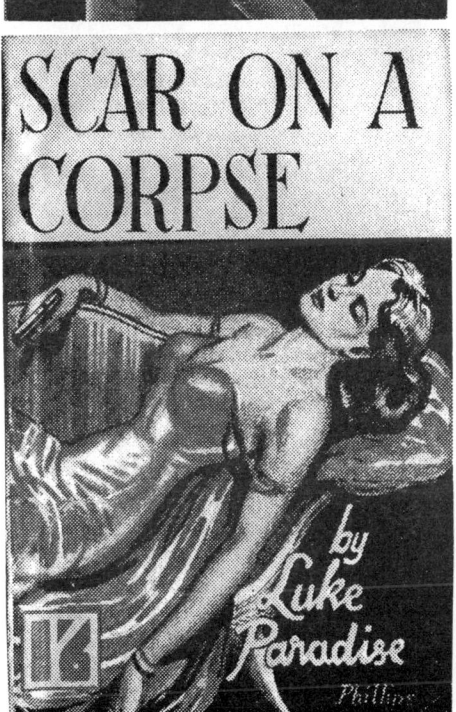

The **Scion** house-name <u>Nat Karta</u> was used by writers Dail Ambler, Donald Cresswell, Norman Lazenby, Victor Norwood, Terry Stanford and even, for one novel (*Vision Sinister*), by John Russell Fearn. The Nat Karta byline was bought by Scion in 1952 (along with Hans Vogel & Hyman Zore) from the Glasgow based publishers Muir-Watson where director John Watson was tired of "churning out that kind of crap....", no matter how well it sold!

Big Top Dame, G453, 1952, vg++, **£20**

Brother Rat, #37099, 1952, Roger Davis cover, writer Vic Norwood, fine, **£25**

Pseudonym <u>Luke Paradise</u> was used on three Scion novels in 1951-52.

Scar on a Corpse, 1951, Phillips cover, vg+, **£20**

Ricky Drayton was a pen-name used by Michael Barnes, who also wrote for Scion as Karl Medusa. Barnes wrote many of his novels whilst travelling around Europe.

It Doesn't Add Up!, 1952, nr vg+, £20

Hells Belles, #42899, 1953, vg+, £20

Most of Scion's gangster output consisted of 128 page novels produced on cheap paper, staplebound, with thin paper covers, typical of all their competitors of the period.

Don't Tempt Me by Sammy Coburn was published in 1951, vg+, £20

Sammy Coburn is thought to be a name used by Bevis Winter. Winter also wrote several hardback crime novels under the name "Peter Cagney" and had novels reprinted under Brown Watson's "Digit" imprint in the late 1950s & early 1960s.

Come out with your hands up!

by HANS LUGER

A SCION 1/6 AMERICAN THRILLER

YOU DON'T SAY!

by HANS LUGAR

A SCION 1/6 PUBLICATION

What Comes Next!

HANS VOGEL

SCION 1/6 AMERICAN THRILLER

Some Get It

BRAD SHANNON

SCION 1/6 AMERICAN THRILLER

Previous page:

A variety of Scion's top gangster team! Including the tough Germanic sounding US writers Hans Luger and Hans Vogel and Vic Hansen as Brad Shannon.

Come Out With Your Hands Up! by Hans Luger, 1951, vg++, **£20**

You Don't Say! By Luger, 1951, cover by Gilmore, vg+, **£20**

What Comes Next, #514/4/53, 1953, vg++, **£25**

Some Get It by Brad Shannon, #515-4-53, 1953, vg++, **£20**

<u>This page:</u>

Dail Ambler was one of few female writers. She wrote the <u>**Danny Spade**</u> novels.

Story of a Killer, features killer Eddie Rixen and gangster Johnny Romano, 1952, vg-, **£10**

The by-line <u>**Nick Perelli**</u> was first introduced in 1949 by Bolton author George Dawson. Dawson initially self-published the novels via Tempest Publications. He soon became a prolific writer for Archer Press as Michael Storme and left his publishing business to partner Thomas H Lane. Writer Thomas Martin continued the Perelli stories. In 1952 Lane sold Perelli to Scion, where Martin continued to write under the by-line.

The tangled web became further complicated when Milestone was launched in 1953. Dawson reclaimed the rights to the pseudonym and sold them to Milestone. Dawson was prepared to share the name with Martin, but Martin preferred to launch his own pseudonym with them as Max Risco

Who Told The Belle, G448, 1953, vg+, cover by Renul, **£20**

There is *HIGH TENSION PLOT* and *INTRIGUING ATMOSPHERE* in...

UNEASY ALIBI

NAT KARTA

A NEW SCION DETECTIVE - 2/-

They Say I'm Bad!

SCION
AMERICAN THRILLER
1'6

BRAD SHANNON

YOU SLAY ME

Danny Spade

1/6

I'LL GET BY!

AMERICAN THRILLER
1 6

FRANK HANSEN

Jealousy

"Hell knows no fury—"

Nat Karta

(3,000,000 COPIES SOLD)

al bocca says Deliver The Body

2/- U.K.

GOOD! It's A Milestone

PARDON MY PISTOL

BRAM CASSON

LID OF THE UNDERWORLD

Previous Page: Scion tough gangster writers

Uneasy Alibi by Nat Karta, 1954, near vg, **£10**

They Say I'm Bad by Brad Shannon, 1953, g++, **£5**

You Slay Me by Danny Spade, Ferrai cover, vg-, **£8**

I'll Get By by Frank Hansen, #40899, 1953, Roger Davis cover, svg, **£10**

This page:

Jealousy by Nat Karta, Scion, 1953, vg-, **£5** (very Monroe like cover girl!)

Deliver The Body by Al Bocca, Milestone #1053, 1953, g++, **£5**

Pardon My Pistol by Bram Casson, Gannet Press (of 37a Kensington Highs St, London, W8), vg-, **£8**

Both Milestone and later Gannet benefited from the break-up of Scion, using many of Scion's authors.

Milestone Publications was based at 98 Great Russell St, London. They were set up by ex-Scion editors and also employed many Scion authors. This gave many authors the chance to sell their own by-lines to another publisher, Milestone also paid higher rates than Scion. Scion re-launched with better deals for authors, they also stopped the use of pen-names owned by them. These included **Nat Karta** and the SF by-line, used by Tubb & Fearn, Volsted Gridban. Milestone were late entrants to this publishing bonanza and by mid 1954, with the collapse of the British pocket book market, both Milestone and Scion went into liquidation.

The Frail's A Phoney, #N2/1008, 1953, vg++, **£25**

Private Eyeful, 1953, vg, **£15**

Scion pseudonym Ricky Drayton also lived on at Milestone.

Nothing To Lose, #1042, 1953, svg, **£15**

BUILD ME A BLONDE

AL BOCCA

MILESTONE 2/- BOOKS U.K.

Was it murder by mistake?

MAKE IT MURDER

AL BOCCA

MILESTONE 2/- BOOKS U.K.

al bocca says

Desire After Dark

2/-

Al Bocca's sales now top 600,000 copies

Bevis Winter, the ex-editor of Stag magazine, was behind the pen-name **Al Bocca**. In this case writing for Milestone rather than Scion. Milestone initially flourished as increasing paper supplies enabled them to sell to a book starved public. By poaching existing by-lines and speed-writing authors they could acquire sufficient storylines as well as paper. By the mid fifties the gangster market became saturated. With the availability of higher quality US sourced novels from Gold Medal etc. and inroads by quality publishers, Penguin, Pan, Transworld and others, the mushroom publishers either radically changed or perished.

Build Me A Blonde, 1953, nr fine, **£20**

Make It Murder, 1953, vg+, **£20**

Desire After Dark, #1026, 1953, vg+, **£20**

A selection of Milestone authors.

Unknown writer **Jack Cairo** produced at least four novels in 1953.

Millionaire Doll, #1010, vg+, £20

Johnny Dark pseudonym of **Victor Norwood** was used for eight novels in the 1953/54 period. Norwood wrote over 330 books before his death in 1983. He appeared to lead an exotic lifestyle as boxer, bank guard, gold & diamond prospector, wrestler, croupier and private eye. He travelled the world and wrote his autobiography together with many other books on travel and prospecting. His most collectable books are the "Tarzanesque" Jacare series for Scion, each worth £30+.

Dame on the Lam, #1000. vg++, £25

Mickey Delaney appeared on two Milestone books in 1953.

Protection For A Lady, nr fine, £20

I SPIT ON YOUR GRAVE

GRIFF
S.S. CRIME REPORTER

2/-

" GRIFF "
TOTAL SALES
750,000
COPIES

You won't be able to miss one word of this searing tale of a "White Negro" and his appalling urge to degrade and slay white-skinned girls.

Terrifically Outspoken

TRAGEDIES of MONTMARTRE

2/- THE OLDEST PROFESSION EXPOSED

BEECH on the BOULEVARD

BY THE AUTHOR OF SIDEWALK FLOOZIE

2/3

Modern Fiction Ltd. was run by Eddie Turvey out of offices at Morwell St, London. Turvey and his wife, Irene had been importing and distributing during the war years and in 1945 started publishing. The huge success of writer Frank Dubrez Fawcett's Ben Sarto novels from 1946 onwards, stoked the demand for further gangster yarns. In 1948 Turvey retained Ernest Lionel McKeag to write tough gangster novels as "Griff" with great titles like "Some Rats Have Two Legs" and "From Dance Hall to Opium Dive". McKeag was an experienced writer (using the pen-name Roland Vane).

Tragedies of Montmartre by Rene Laroche, cover by FT, nr vg+, **£20**

I Spit on Your Grave by Griff, nrvg+, **£20** (about the ill-used negro population of the Deep South of the USA)

Beech on the Boulevard by Ben Sarto, vg+, **£20**

In 1950, **Edwin Self**, co-director at Curtis Warren and ex-editor at Hamilton & Co formed his own company. He published French titillation novels, gangsters, sci-fi, war and westerns. Several house-names were used for the gangster material including Pete Costello, Max Conlon, Maurice Dekobra and Bart Banarto.

Self was based at 42 Greys Inn Road, Holburn and his writers included Maurice Tessier, Albert Garrett, Lisle Willis and George Bell, many following Self from Curtis Warren. Bell and Self were to spend time in gaol in 1954 for publishing obscene libel in the form of five novels (a Paul Valois, a Bart Banarto and three Pete Costello novels).

Self was one of the most dogged of the mushroom publishers, despite gaol he survived the mid 50s publishing crash.

On his release from prison in 1955 he continued to publish, initially with war novels and then in 1957 formed (the now very collectible imprint) Pedigree Books, publishing juvenile delinquency novels by Hal Ellson and US sourced horror and occult as well as sensationalist true crime stories.

Dames Play Dumb by Bart Banarto 1951, vg+ (other than price alterations!) **£10**

Crime City by Bart Banarto, 1952?, fine, **£20**

both by **Bart Banarto**, who "grew up on the sidewalks of the Eastside of New York" and learned the "facts of life in a hard and tough school."

In reality Banarto was a pseudonym used by Albert Garrett and others.

Marc Lavelle (author of Reefer Girl), was somewhat of a cross-over between the sexy french romances and the gangster low-life story. Pete Costello dished up out and out low-life crime describing the "seamy side of American gangsterdom ... rackets and hoodlums... the inside on 'dope' .. the brutality of gangsters and the sordid lives of their molls and floozies". And Pete should know, since he "grew up during the roaring twenties". (True, but exactly where did he grow up, and was the experience relevent?)

Curves Spell Death by Marc Lavelle, 1952?, fine **£20**

Undercover Dame by Pete Costello, 1952?, fine, **£20**

Moll For A Morgue by Pete Costello, 1952?, svg, **£15**

All published by Edwin Self

Hamilton & Co. (Stafford) Ltd., one of the most prolific of the mushroom publishers, was launched in 1943. The directors were Henry Assael and Joseph Pacey. Their first novel was published in 1945 with much of the early romance, western and gangster output written by Norman Wesley Firth.

Hamiltons use their logo of "We Never Publish A Dull Story" for the gangster novels above (that don't rely on good girl cover art).

Homicide Racket by Clifton Rank, nrvg+, **£10**

Rostron Outfit in Chicago by Dean Morgan, 1952, nrvg+, **£10**

Why Call It Homicide? by Ross Kirby, 1950, nrvg+, **£12**

The Rostron outfit were featured in at least six other gangster books and then suddenly switched to a western scenario.

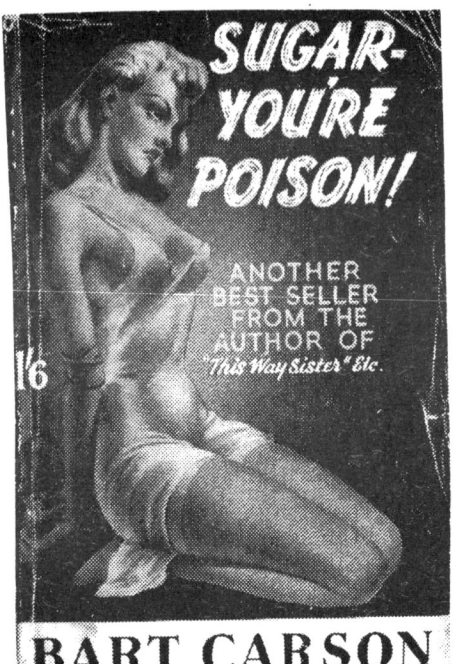

Hamiltons were initially based at Melville Court and then Goldhawk Rd, London W12. In 1949 Gordon Landsborough became editor, production manager and writer and was immediately "shocked by the deplorably low standard of story-telling". Landsborough advertised for writers of westerns, gangsters & SF and recruited some "quality" authors like Leonard Barnard, Richard Conroy, Graham Fisher, James McCormick, William Maconachie, Norman Robson and Harry Hossent. In 1955 Hamiltons launched the Panther imprint, still in use recently.

Sugar- You're Poison by Bart Carson, vg £15 (Bondage cover)

Honey Stay Blonde by Jeff Bogar, 1952?, svg, £10

Death Smells of Cordite by Mike McCracken, vg, £10

The McCracken pen-name was also used on a number of western novels.

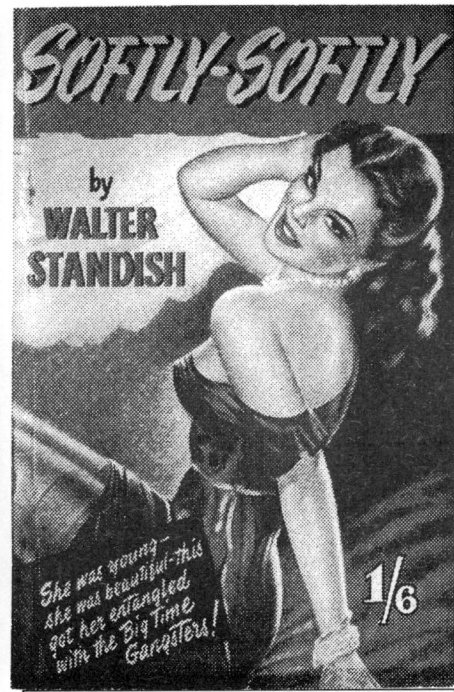

Brown Watson was started in 1943 by Bernard & Sadie Babani (who were also directors of Instructive Arts). In 1945 under the new guidance of Albert and Solomon Babani the company moved into fiction publishing. They were based at The Grampians, Western Gate, London, W6. They are the last survivors of the mushroom publishers, still publishing chidrens fiction today.

In 1955 they obtained manuscripts from Fiction House to supplement their successful western novels and in 1956 acquired further novels from the now defunct Dragon Press (some from John Russell Fearn under pseudonyms).

Floosie Takes A Fall, vg, £15

Softly-Softly, 1952, svg, £15

Don't Sell Me Cheap, svg, £15

All by house-name of Curtis gangster novels, **Walter Standish**

Walter Standish may not have been the raciest sounding author's name around but he was adept at exposing the nightlife of Paris or America (you know what I mean!). The **Instructive Arts** to **Brown Watson** connection made with Standish writing for both outfits. Or maybe you can do better? If so write sending your MSS to Brown Watson who "pay approved rates".

Whatever the reason, Brown Watson survived the over-production problems of 1953-54 that led to the demise of rival publishers Curtis Warren and Scion Ltd.

Women That Are Lost published by Instructive Arts (London), svg, **£10**

Crazy Dame, Brown Watson, vg+ **£20**

Weep Not My Darling, Brown Watson, vg++, **£20**

All by Walter Standish

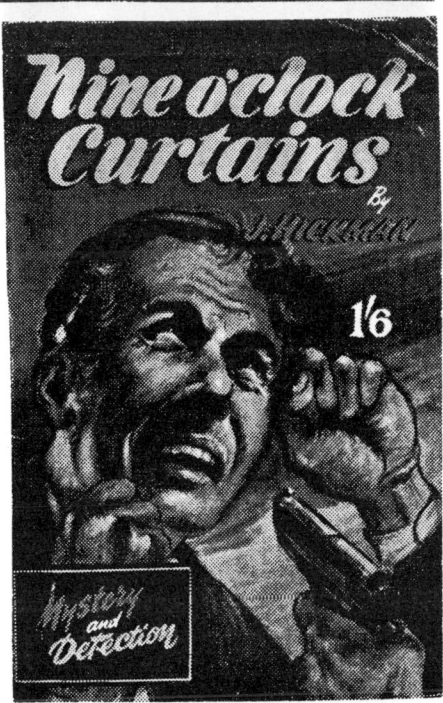

Rex Richards was another pen-name used by **Brown Watson** for its gangster books. By 1953 the gangster novel was on the wane and Curtis Warren rejigged their range, changing the format, covers and introducing other genre fiction like historical novels, lost world exploration, aero fiction and foreign legion novels.

Westerns and war stories continued successfully but 1956 saw a change of address and the new imprint of Digit Books. Digit continued to publish war, crime, romance and many SF originals besides reprinting titles by Edgar Wallace and Leslie Charteris amongst others, but now in the more familiar paperback size.

Women At Dusk by Rex Richards, vg++, £20

Madame Don't Be Difficult by Clark Loman, (Cover by Kris), vg+, £20

Nine O'Clock Curtains by J Hickman, vg+, £15

A BULLET FOR
THE COUNTESS
by SYDNEY
HORLER

Horler for Excitement

1/6

1/6

SYDNEY HORLER'S

An exciting story – full of action, suspense & drama.

GREAT NEW THRILLER
OF THE UNDERWORLD

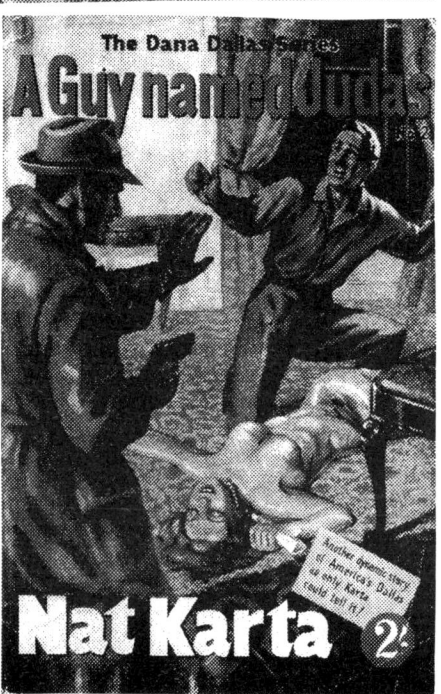

The Dana Dallas Series

A Guy named Judas

Another dynamic story of America's Dallas as only Karta could tell it!

Nat Karta

2/-

This Page: Sydney Horler's thrillers were popular from the 1930s to 1950s, alongside other mainstream writers like Edgar Wallace, EP Oppenheim, Sapper etc. Brown Watson (London) were the unlikely reprinters in 1950 of his 1945 & 1947 novels respectively. Both are scarce.

A Bullet For The Countess, svg,£10

The Corridors of Fear, vg, £10

The unconnected Muir -Watson of Glasgow published:

A Guy Named Judas by Nat Karta, (Dana Dallas No2), 1952, vg+, £15

Next Page:

For Men Only by Beth Brown, Perl cover, Streamline, g++, £6

Some Dame!! by Nat Karta, Scion Gangster No 41999, 1953, g+, £6

No Dame Wants To Die by Max Clinten, Moring, g++, £6

Play It Smart by Steve Markham, Gaywood, g+, £6

FOR MEN ONLY

BETH BROWN

1/6

STREAMLINE SOPHISTICATED

Some Dame!!

NAT KARTA

SCION
AMERICAN THRILLER
1/6

No dame wants to die

2/-

MAX CLINTEN

STEVE MARKHAM'S

PLAY IT SMART

STREAMLINE AMERICAN GANGSTER STORY

81

Hamilton & Co's director Joseph Pacey set up **Curtis Warren** in 1948 with Edwin Self (ex-Hamilton's). Curtis realised the potential of the genres of tough crime, western and science fiction. The prolific Dennis Talbot Hughes wrote much of their early output, often at a rate of a book each week. Frederick Foden wrote many gangsters as Brett Vane, Nick Baroni et al, whilst much of the western output was written by John Jennison (who later novelised many of the Gerry Anderson TV programmes). In 1952 Curtis began issuing SF & Westerns simultaneously in hardback for library use, these are tough to find in condition.

Bait by Lane Martin (Perl cover?) was published in 1951 nrvg+ **£15**

Look Down For Mercy by Max Gordon (1952), svg-nrvg+ **£15**

Make Mine Murder by Bevis Winter (1950), svg **£15**

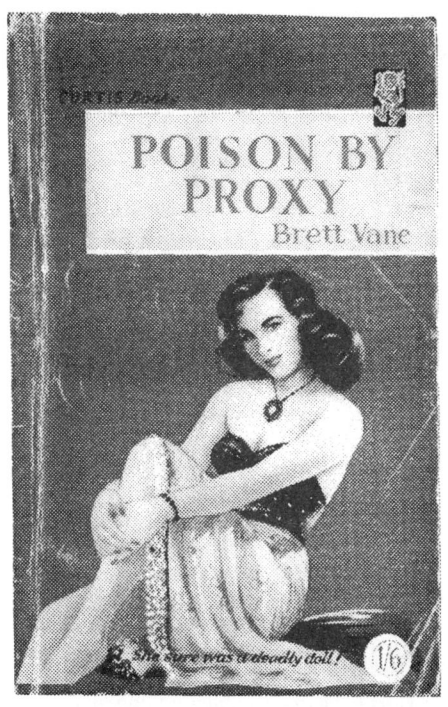

The mysterious **FT** was one of the best of the "gangster" artists. His use of colour and action was excellent, witness the examples in this book. He painted for John Spencer and Curtis Warren, but most of his work can be seen on gangsters from Kaye Publications.

This page illustrates a mixed bag from **Curtis Warren**.

Detective Crime Stories by Lee Dexter, 1949, FT cover, (book also includes two stories by Bevis Winter, The Ghoul and Pickle Profit), svg-vg+, **£15**

Poison by Proxy, by Brett Vane (author unknown), 1953, vg-, **£6**

Strike Midnight by Bruce Kelland, 1954, vg-, **£5**

As can be seen from these Curtis' artwork can be very patchy. This applies especially to their extensive Sci Fi output in the 1950s.

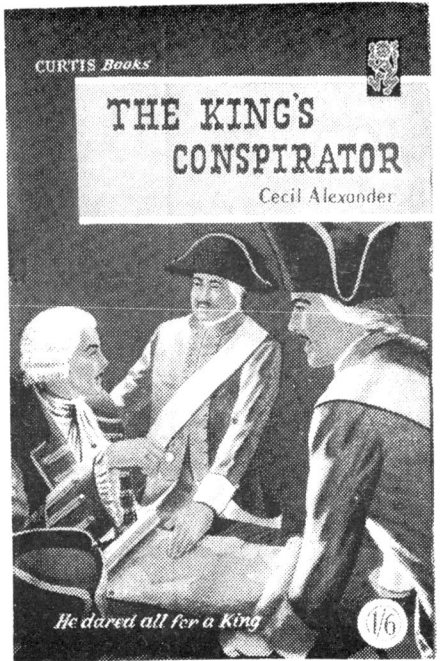

Curtis Warren published the usual "mushroom" fare of gangsters, sexy romances, westerns and sci-fi. Whilst the quality of writing and cover art could often leave much to be desired they were prepared to try something different. Like Spencers and Hamiltons, they tried to cash on foreign legion films like "Beau Geste", like Scion and Spencers they produced jungle adventure stories to cash in on the success of "Tarzan". But Curtis went much further trying Aerofiction genres and **Cecil Alexander**'s historical fiction. The latter only ran to four books (in 1954, the year that Curtis expired) and was probably part of a vain attempt to boost flagging sales.

The King's Creditor, svg, £6

The King's Conspirator, vg+, £6

The King's Cupbearers, vg+, £6

All featured Simon Murray an exiled Jacobite swordsman adventurer perhaps inspired by the success of Orczy's Scarlet Pimpernel.

An exciting drama of crime and intrigue

THE UNSUSPECTED

A M Crime Novel

MICHAEL BARNES 1/-

THEY KILL TO LIVE

Mark Shane

2/-

DON'T CRY NOW

HANK JANSON

TEN MILLION SALE

2/6

Alexander Moring had been in existence as a publisher since 1903. In 1951 it was taken over by Martin Secker and Graeme Hutchinson.

On release from prison in 1955 (for publishing obscene Hank Janson novels), **Reginald Carter** bought the company. Despite his problems, the lure of easy money prompted Carter to revive Janson, publishing new novels and reprinting some of the older ones. Many were printed in France to avoid the threat of legal action. Alongside the new look (yellow & red stripe) Jansons, Carter also published gangsters by Mark Shane, Darcy Glinto and David Steel. He also reprinted (as at Gaywood) US Authors Edward Ronns and Gil Brewer plus a few highly collectable Harlan Ellison JD novels.

The Unsuspected by Michael Barnes, svg, **£8**

They Kill to Live, Mark Shane, 1956,vg, **£8**

(Sadie) **Don't Cry Now**, Hank Janson, 1957, fine, **£6**

MAKE MINE
BEAUTIFUL

**MICHAEL
STORME**

Author of "Unlucky Virgin", "Make Mine a Shroud"
and "Make Mine a Harlot"

MAKE MINE A
VIRGIN

by

**MICHAEL
STORME**

Author of "Unlucky Virgin"
"Make Mine a Shroud"
"Make Mine a Harlot"
"Make Mine Beautiful"

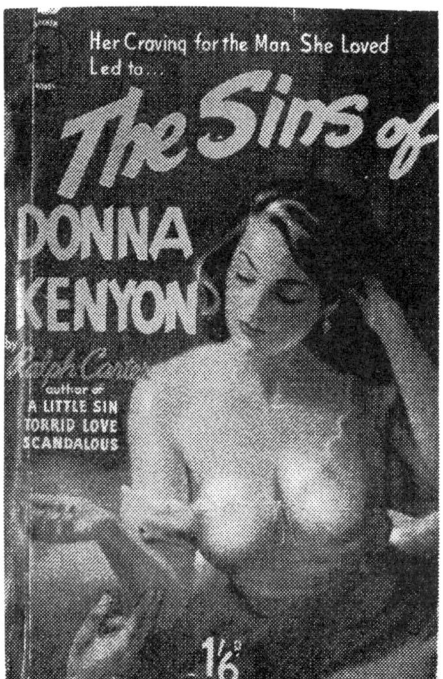

Her Craving for the Man She Loved
Led to...

The Sins of
DONNA
KENYON

by
Ralph Carter
author of
A LITTLE SIN
TORRID LOVE
SCANDALOUS

The prolific publishing house of_R& L Locker incorporating Harborough and Archer Press published many popular gangster authors as well as the Renin/Vane type sexy romances.

Michael Storme (George Dawson) was amongst the most popular and when teamed with a John Pollack girly cover made a formidable combination. "Make Mine Beautiful" employs the the blurb "a tempest of thrills for the reader" and it was as Nick Perelli that Dawson started Tempest Publications in 1949.

Make Mine Beautiful by Michael Storme, Archer, 1949, Pollack cover, vg++, £20

Make Mine A Virgin by Michael Storme, Archer, 1949, Pollack cover, fine, £20 - Both Stormes are Catastrophe novels about atomic plans etc.

The Sins of Donna Kenyon by Ralph Carter, Archer, svg-vg+, £15

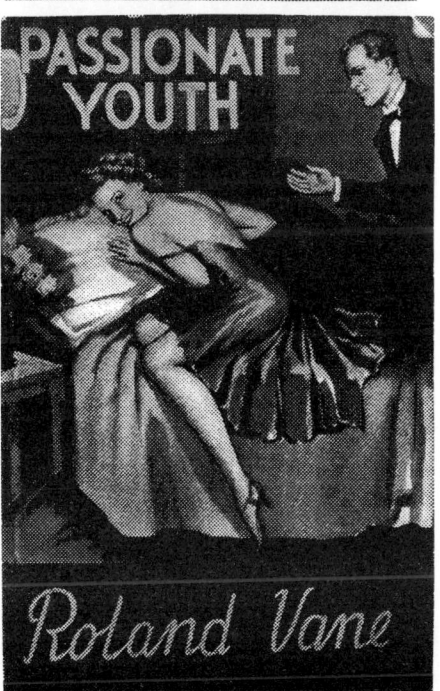

Roland Vane (Ernest McKeag) and Paul Renin (Richard Goyne) made up much of the early output of the Locker/Archer stable. Vane was the author of such classic books as "White Slaves of New Orleans" and "Night Haunts of Paris" as well as other such "french-flavoured" novels.

Cover art was of a high standard with Heade and Perl used extensively plus the excellent artwork from another "Headelike" hand as shown above.

Woman with a Past by Roland Vane, Archer Press, 1949, vg+, **£25**

Wanton Wife by Roland Vane, Archer Press, 1949, vg+, **£25**

Passionate Youth by Roland Vane, R&L Locker, 1948, Perl cover, nrvg+, **£10**.

The Lockers were to survive the difficult mid fifties to launch Ace Books in 1957.

Paul Renin was **R&L Locker**'s most prolific author. Behind the name was Richard Goyne one time successful journalist turned author. Renin was first published by Federation Press in 1924. Arthur Gray and Frederick Mowl launched Gramol in 1928. As one of Britain's earlier adult publishers by 1930 their lusty french Renin tales had landed Gray and Mowl in Wormwood Scrubs.

Gramol ceased publishing in 1937 (Gray continued after the war with Phoenix, whilst his son Barrington formed his own company operating alongside Phoenix and Popular Publications).

In 1946 the Lockers established a deal with Arthur Gray to reprint Renin novels (Lockers were already distributing Renins published by Phoenix).

This Page: Heads! I Marry You by Paul Renin, R&L Locker, 1947, cover by Phillip Simmonds, vg+, **£15**

Mark Amery's Mistress by Paul Renin, Archer Press, 1952, g++, **£8**

Overleaf: Despite a diet of primarily sexploitation and gangster novels, the Lockers did experiment with westerns in the early days of the Archer imprint. Traditional authors like Lee Floren and Charles H Snow were used with excellent artwork from Heade and Charles McConnell amongst others.

Trail End by Lee Floren, McConnell cover, vg++, **£10**

Wild Border Guns by Lee Floren, Heade cover, vg++, **£30**

The Indiscreet Confessions of a Nice Girl, Archer, 1951, vg (Keyhole cover), **£10**

Ladies Sleep Alone by Lew Della, Kaywin, 1951, vg++, **£15**

TRAIL END

LEE FLOREN

WESTERN AMERICAN SERIES

Wild Border Guns

LEE FLOREN

'AMERICA'S ACE WESTERN WRITER'

The Best Gangster Story Yet!

2/6
PRICE IN U.S.A. AND CANADA 35¢

LADIES SLEEP ALONE
by Lew Della

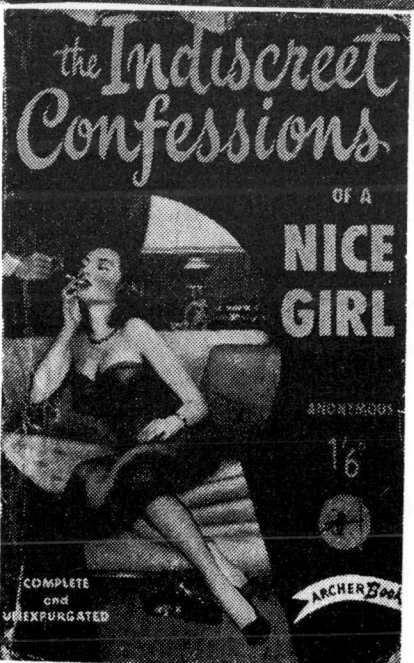

the Indiscreet Confessions OF A NICE GIRL

ANONYMOUS

1/6

COMPLETE and UNEXPURGATED

ARCHER Book

This Page:

Girls For Sale by Nick Baroni, Curtis Warren, vg+, **£15**

Big Time Girl by Nick Baroni, Curtis Warren, vg, **£10**

Dames Meet Death by Len Cooper (title page says Johnny Death), Vauser & Wils (London) Ltd, 161 Pentonville Rd, N1, svg, **£10**

Next Page:

The Right To Motherhood by Bree Narran, Camden Publishing (323 Upper St, London N1), Perl cover?, vg++. **£5**

L'Assommoir by Emil Zola, Camden Publishing, svg, **£8**

The Web of Desire by D L'Arnaud, D McKenzie, Glasgow, 1949?, vg-, **£5**

None Should Look by Robert Kingston, MC Publishing, 1950, Glasgow, fine, **£10** - story of murder.

Both based at 2 Southpark Terrace.

The
RIGHT TO
MOTHERHOOD

BREE NARRAN

THE
WEB OF DESIRE

D. L'ARNAUD

1/6

L'ASSOMMOIR

By
Emile Zola

NONE
SHOULD LOOK

ROBERT
KINGSTON

35¢

1/-

M. E. PUBLICATIONS

This Page: A Miscellany

Death Wears A Green Hat by Will Creed, published by Walter Edwards, London, 1946, vg+ dw, **£10**

Information Received by Peter Cheyney, Bantam Books, London (Todd Publishing), 1948, cover by C.MAC, vg++, **£15**

Savage Love by Whit Harrison (Harry Whittington), Paladin Press, London, SE1, 1952, vg++, published in US as Original Book 718 (Belarski cover), **£50**

Next Page: More Miscellaneous

Yellow Babe by Ace Capelli, Kaye Publications, WC1, 1951?, g++, **£5**

Memory & Desire by Leonora Hornblow, WH Allen, 1950, svg, **£5**

They Kill to Live by Mark Shane, Comyns (139 Borough High St, London SE1), 1953, vg+, **£10**

Road Floozie by Darcy Glinto, Robin Hood Press, 1950, svg, **£10**

YELLOW BABE

AMERICAN GANGSTER STORY

1/6

...CE CAPELLI

UNABRIDGED EDITION OF THE FAMOUS NOVEL
ORIGINALLY PUBLISHED AT 9'6

Memory and Desire

LEONORA HORNBLOW

1/6

THEY KILL TO LIVE

Mark Shane

2/

GLINTO REVEALS GRIM TRUTHS IN FICTION FORM

ROAD FLOOZIE

by Darcy Glinto

2/

This page:

A Private Killing by Howard Kent, Cooper Books, (291/293 Grays Inn Rd, London, WC1), 1953, vg++, **£20**

A Coffin For Clara by Brett Diamond, John Spencer (Shepherd Bush Rd, London, W6), 1950, vg+, **£15**

Rostron Outfit in Rio by Dean Morgan, Hamilton, 1952, vg, **£10**

Next Page: In 1924 Paul Renin's first romance The Brute was published. Trident books were still reprinting this and others in the early 1960s!

Wedding Night published by Verlock Press (as Trident book), vg+, **£5**

The Brute, Verlock Press (Trident), fine, **£5**

Lonely Wives, Verlock Press (Trident), fine, **£5**

Man Mad, Phoenix Press, Simmonds cover?, 1950s rp?, fine, **£10**

WEDDING
NIGHT

PAUL
RENIN

2'6

THE
BRUTE

PAUL
RENIN

2'6

Lonely Wives

Paul
Renin

2'6

MAN
MAD

by
Paul
Rénin

Passion and
Excitement were
the sum total of
her being

2/6

Love in Peril by Eileen Wilmot, Piccadilly 9d novel published by Fiction House, 54 Fleet Street, London. (Sophisticated cigarette-smoking dame leads us through death & mystery), 1947, vg, £8

Dangerous Dames by N Wesley Firth, cover by Perl, Grant Hughes, 1948?, vg++, £20

Murder At The Bookstall by Henry Holt, Mellifont Press M26, 1956, svg, £10, (looks like the argument started over who got to the Heade paperback first!). Mellifont produced many hundreds of paperback novels between the 1930s & 1960s. Their heyday was in the 1930s & 1940s, but they did well with Nat Gould's Horseracing novels in the 1950s.

In 1963 <u>**Gold Star Books**</u> started to reprint many of the Hank Janson novels in the USA

IL7-11 **Kill Her With Passion** (Crowns Can Kill), cover by Barton, fine **£10**

IL7-12 **Lover** (She Wolf), cover by Maguire, fine **£10**

IL7-13 **Brazen Seductress** (Ripe For Rapture), cover by Maguire, fine **£10**

IL7-13 **A Nice Way To Die** (Mastermind), cover by Rader, fine **£10**

IL7-14 **It's Bedtime Baby!** (Cutie On Call), cover by Barton, fine, **£10**

IL7-15 **Hell's Angels** (Late Night Revel), cover by Maguire, fine, **£10**

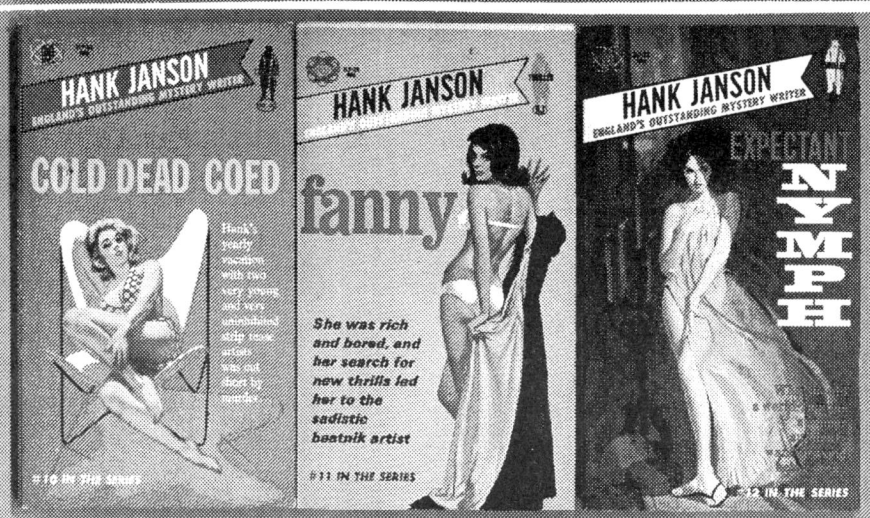

This wasn't the first time that Hank had been exported to the USA, in 1949 Checkerbooks of New York published Lady Mind That Corpse (Heade, worth £35)

IL7-17 **Hot House** (Venus Makes Three), cover by Barton, 1964, fine, **£10**

IL7-18 **Passionate Playmates** (Go With A Jerk), cover Maguire, 1964, fine, **£10**

IL7-19 **Her Weapon Is** (Conflict), 1964, fine, **£10**

IL7-20 **Cold Dead Coed** (No Regrets For Clara), cover Barton, 1964, fine, **£10**

IL7-28 **Fanny** (This Dame Dies Soon), cover Barton, 1964, fine, **£10**

IL7-32 **Expectant Nymph** (Murder), cover Maguire, 1964, fine, **£10**

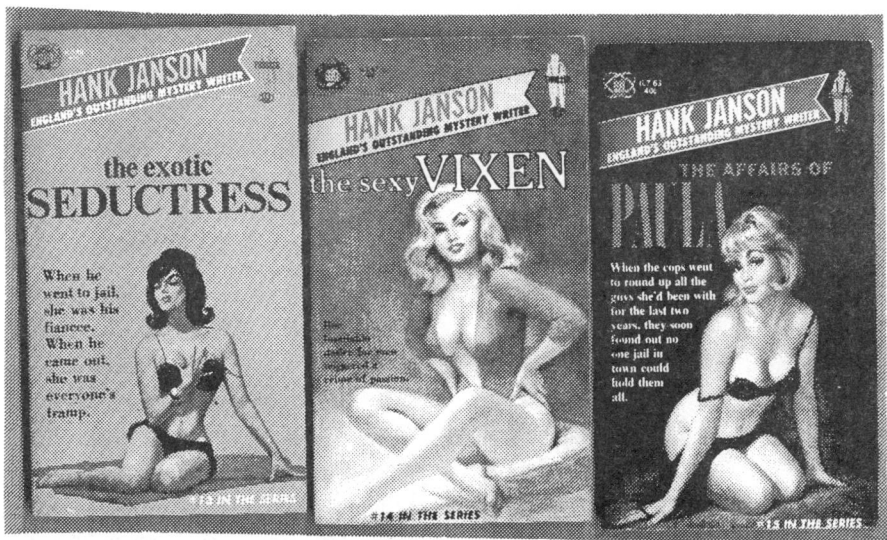

In 1964 **G Gold & D Warburton** owned the rights to the Hank Janson novels. Gold Star books were owned by The New International Library, Derby, Conn., USA. Gold Star published a variety of material including Buffalo Bill novels and Barton Werper's Tarzan pastiche novels (Gold Star ran foul of ERB Inc. with these unauthorised editions, and this may have led to their downfall). Primarily they were a sleaze house with many sexy novels and "factual" books on sex.

The <u>Gold Star</u> series ran to seventeen titles before the demise of Gold Star in 1965.

IL7-48 **The Exotic Seductress** (They Die Alone), cover Barton, 1964, fine, **£10**

IL7-57 **The Sexy Vixen** (Skirts Bring Sorrow), cover Barton, 1964, fine, **£10**

IL7-63 **The Affairs of Paula** (Sweet Fury), cover Barton, 1965, fine, **£10**

IL7-68 **A Nympho Named Sylvia** (Enemy of Men), 1965, fine, **£10**

IL7-70 **Becky** (Sinister Rapture), cover by Maguire, 1965, fine, **£10**

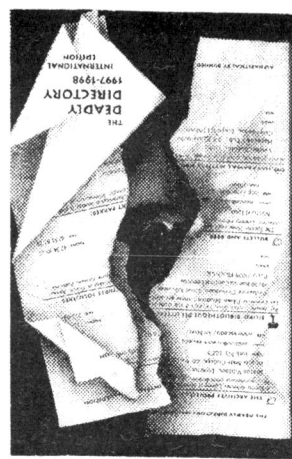

TV Tie-Ins by Kurt Peer. 370+ page Bibliography of American TV Tie-ins by Kurt Peer. Published by Neptune 1997. Master list, indexed by author, publisher, actors, TV Show, episodes etc. Colour cover, some illos. £19.50

Lester Dent- The Man, his craft, his Market by H Martin McCarey-Laird. The story of the greatest pulp writer, creator of Doc Savage. !00+ pages. 1994. £8.95

The Deadly Directory 1997-1998 edition. 150 pages, lists Crime related shops, booksellers, archives, symposiums, theatres, web sites, discussion groups, newsletters, magazines etc, etc. All the contacts needed by crime fan or researcher. £17.95

Paperbacks Pulps & Comics- Volume 4. British magazine devoted to the hobby. 100+ pages, perfect bound, colour cover. #4 contains Doc Savage, Bunduki, EE Doc Smith, Beacon Books, Green Hornet, Space/Horror comics & more. £3.95

Paperbacks USA & UK. Volume 1. Annoted illustrated catalogue of highly collectible British, US & Australian pbs. Colour cover, 44 pages, £3.95

Fantasy Annual #1. Articles of 50s British SF, new stories by Tubb, Bounds, Somers, reprint of Fearn & Fearn/Turner graphic story. 90+ pages, well produced. Published by Cosmos. £5

Paperbacks, Pulps & Comics Volume 3. The British magazine devoted to the hobby. All volumes available, perfect bound 100+ pages, colour cover. #3 contains SF Film tie-ins, The Spider, Richard Allen, McLoughlin, Jeff Hawke etc. Zardoz 1996, new £3.95. **Special catalogue price £3**

Paperback Parade #45, many other issues available. Longest runnibg and currently only US mag devoted to hobby. Colour cover & some inside. WR Burnett, SF paperback art, Australian early SF pbs, Laurence James, Hershman & sleaze etc-,Gryphon 1996, new £5

Paperback, Pulp & Comic Collector #8. Fore runner of Paperbacks, Pulps & Comics. 100+ pages. colour cover. **#8 British artwork edition**, plus Peff, Pat Owen interviews, Dr Who, Creature from Black Lagoon, Gerry Anderdon, Tarzan Comics, Marshall Grover, Challengers of Unknown. as new, **special price £2**. Issues 1-8 available at £2 ea.

Denis McLoughlin, The Master of Light & Shade by Francis Herzberg. Long waited comprehensive guide to McLoughlins work in books & comics. Colour inside & out. 188 pages. Gryphon 1995, new £15

The Harboiled Art of Denis McLoughlin by Ashford & McLoughlin. Denis' own story and Ashford's comprehensive appraisal of DmcL's wotk. Colour inside & out. 80 pages, new £10

Australian Vintage Paperback Guide by Graeme Flanagan. 228 pages & huge body of work. Story & listings of publishers. Many illustrations of great rare covers. Of interest to US, UK & Australasians as do turn up around the world. Colour inside & out. Gryphon 1994. new £15

The Movie Tie-In Book by Moe Wadle. 120 pages lists all US tie-ins known with prices, info etc, some illos.

Glossy cover, nice production. £9.99

Relics of Sherlock Holmes by Gary Lovisi. 58 page booklet. Listing films, plays, pastiches, comic books, fanzines & much more. Illus. Plenty of Holmes material to look for. **£4**

Edgar Rice Burroughs Fantastic Worlds. Huge paperback, 192 pages, colour cover, plenty of illos, quality book. Large number of articles on Burroughs & his worlds, illustrators etc. Great book by James Van Hise. **£14.95**

FROM THE PULPS

INTO PAPERBACKS:

A REFERENCE DOCUMENT

by

Roy G. James

The Good Ship Venus - The Erotic Voyage of the Olympia Press by John De St Jorre. 330 page story of publisher of William Burroughs, De Sade, Donleavy etc. and erotica. Illus, nice book. Pimlioc 1995. **£10**

Amazing Pulp Heroes by Frank Hamilton & Link Hullar. New edition, 200+ pages. Colour dw. All those guys, Doc Savage, Shadow, G8, Tarzan, Kioga plus many more & much on pulps. Illus by Hamilton. **£19.50**

From the Pulps Into Paperbacks. 100 page, colour cover. Lists all pulp appearances that had paperback edition. Shadow, Doc, G8, Tarzan, Spider, plus Best of series (Brown, Asimov etc) plus crime & SF compilations of pulp stories. **£10**

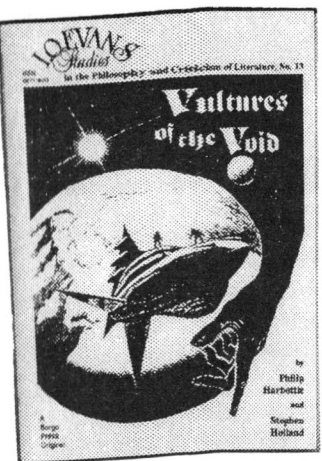

Vultures of the Void by Philip Harbottle and Stephen Holland. A fascinating look at the 50s British, particularly SF publishers. The stories of the publishers writers from Scion, Curtis Warren , Spencers etc. Borgo Press , 1991, new £13.95

The Mushroom Jungle by Steve Holland. 200+ pages telling the story of the rise and fall of postwar British paperback publishing amongst the many "get rich quick", "mushroom" publishers of the 50s. SF, Crime, Wesern, Romance genres and plenty of lurid covers by Heade etc in b&w and colour. Zardoz Books, new. Normaly £14.95, **special offer £10**

British Science Fiction Paperbacks & Magazines 1949-1956, an annoted bibliography and guide by Harbottle & Holland.. Companion volume to Fantastic work, with story resumes, pseudonyms & all artists tracked. 232 pages. Borgo Press, new £15.95

Down The Badger Hole - RL Fanthorpe: The Badger Years by Debbie Cross. Intoduction by David Langford & Lionel Fanthorpe. 164 page Story of how Lionel wrote those characteristic books. Icludes biblio & full length "Curse of Khan", Wrigley Cross Books. new £10

Over My Dead Body by Lee Server. Lavish story of sensational age of Us paperbacks 1945-55 Great book, plenty of illustrations (mostly colour), plus genres crime, drugs, JD, good girl, SF etc. Chronicle Books, new £11.99

Collectable Vintage Paperbacks At Auction 1995 - results from 1991-1994 complete. How do we get our prices, now that the Warren Price Guide is out of print. Well, here's your best bet to those top books! Arranged in Publisher no & key author order, its easty to spot those hot tites. 16, 000 entries, An eyeopener, Gorgon Books, new £15

BOOKS & PERIODICALS ON PAPERBACK COLLECTING

THE MUSHROOM JUNGLE - a history of Postwar Paperback Publishing by Steve Holland has just been nominated for an Anthony Award for best critical work (Bouchercon 26, World Mystery Convention). The book concentrates on British publishers who"mushroomed" out of the WW2 paper shortages to establish a diverse, often lurid paperback culture in the postwar era. The book covers all genres from Crime To Westerns, from Sci-Fi to Romance, and has a large section featuring the infamous Hank Janson Obscenity trial. Extensively illustrated it is available from the publishers Zardoz Books for £14.95 or from Gary Lovisi at Gryphon Publications in the USA.

VULTURES OF THE VOID by Philip Harbottle & Stephen Holland is the definitive story of British Science Fiction Publishing from 1946-1956. All the publishers, authors, artists etc. Of interest also to general & crime pb fans, has info on all "Mushroom Publishers". Published by Borgo, 1992. £13.95

BRITISH SCIENCE FICTION Paperbacks & Magazines, by Philip Harbottle & Stephen Holland 1949-1956, an annoted bibliography & guide, gives all book story-lines, pseudonyms etc., well indexed, invaluable book. Borgo Press 1995, £15.95

PAPERBACKS, PULPS & COMICS: is published by Zardoz Books and is the UK's is now over 140 pages long and is published about twice a year. Its currently the only European magazine specialising in this area. Several articles on "Mushroom Publishers"Issues are £3.95 plus £0.50 postage (UK & Europe, USA & elsewhere £1).

PAPERBACK PARADE: is Gary Lovisi's collectors magazine, published bimonthly with colour covers. It contains 100+ pages full of news, interviews, letters, info, articles,and dozens of reproductions of collectible paperback covers, many with articles on British pbs. It's the longest- running publication in the hobby and is available at $6 per issue, subscriptions: 6 issues for $30 ($36 outside USA) from Gryphon Publications, PO Box 209, Brooklyn, NY 11228-0209, USA. In the UK & Europe it can also be obtained from Zardoz Books (£5.50 incl. p&p).

CRIMETIME magazine published by Oldcastle Books has several articles on gangster paperbacks and paperback artists. £2.50

PBO the newsletter of the British Association of Paperback Collectors, much of this is written by Stephen Holland and many articles relate to the mushroom publishers, authors & artists. Specifically Issue 2-3 is about R&L Locker, Gramol, Richard Goyne/Paul Renin. £3 to non-members. Contact Steve Holland, 105 Lexden Rd, Colchester, Essex, CO3 3RB.

OFFICIAL PRICE GUIDE TO PAPERBACKS by Jon Warren (House of Collectibles, lst ed. 1991) a 900 page listing of most US pbs published from 1939 to about 1970 with prices. Good basic information, though I'd take the prices with a pinch of salt.

HANCER'S PRICE GUIDE TO PAPERBACKS by Kevin Hancer (Wallace-Homested, 3rd ed. 1990) another price guide, overlaps with Warren, another good basic guide to what is available with a good author index.

OVER MY DEAD BODY by Lee Server (Chronicle Books, 1994) is a fine overview of US vintage paperbacks with many gorgeous colour and b&w reproductions of scarce collectible paperbacks (some mention of Reginald Heade).

PAPERBACKS USA by Piet Schreuders (Blue Dolphin(USA), Virgin (UK), 1981) an excellent look at the art and artists who did the classic covers on American paperbacks.

UNDERCOVER by Thomas Bonn (Penguin Books, 1982) a fine history and study of the paperback publishing field with many covers shown in colour (mainly US).